KV-512-992

Contents

Introduction   **v**

Stagecraft   **1**

  The Stage   1
  Scenery   6
  Methods of Staging   7
  Set Pieces   10
  Designing Scenery   13
  Arena Scenery   18
  Making Scenery   19
  Painting   38
  Putting Scenery Together   44
  Properties   52
  Using Plastic, Foam, and Metal Onstage   54
  Stage Lighting   59
  Sound Systems   78
  Sound Effects   80
  Stage and Lighting Terminology   86
  Suggested Activities   89
  Bibliography   91

THIRD EDITION

Stagecraft

Roy A. Beck
Western Michigan University

National Textbook Company
a division of NTC *Publishing Group* • Lincolnwood, Illinois USA

To my father, Rudy Beck, who was always building something for someone; from whom I learned the meaning of craftsmanship.

Cover photo: Eric Futran, Marilyn Gartman Agency, Chicago

1991 Printing

Published by National Textbook Company, a division of NTC Publishing Group.
© 1990 by NTC Publishing Group, 4255 West Touhy Avenue,
Lincolnwood (Chicago), Illinois 60646-1975 U.S.A.
Library of Congress Catalog Card Number: 88-60944

1 2 3 4 5 6 7 8 9 ML 9 8 7 6 5 4 3 2

792.02

030845

20.8.96.

Introduction

Stagecraft is the art of planning, building, and coordinating all the elements necessary to create the setting the playwright describes. This revised edition of *Stagecraft* is a how-to volume—how to design, construct, light, prop, and sound a show.

We are all builders of some kind. Producing a play requires several kinds of building. Acting requires building a character aside from your own personality. Scene design requires building mental images for the set in which actors can develop their characterizations. Scene construction, lighting props, and sound complete the mental images of the playwright, designer, and director. Play production also involves building within yourself. As you learn the skills of carpentry or electrical or sound engineering, you learn how you can develop those skills, and how your confidence increases as you use them.

The arts of the theatre are practical—you must experience them. No textbook can adequately convey the experience of building your first flat, making your first prop, or running lights or sound. You must work hands-on to understand and come to own these skills.

The methods described in *Stagecraft* are by no means the only ones. These are the methods I have learned, created, used, and taught to my students. They worked for those who taught me, they have worked for me, and they can work for you. Different methods may produce the same effect or a new and different effect. As you learn, you can adapt methods to achieve a desired effect. It is essential, however, that you command the basic methods before adapting them.

It is not possible to acknowledge all of the students who have helped build my sets in the past 30 years, but they will recognize their contributions to this volume. I thank them for their immediate help on the productions they worked on, and also for their help in refining the crafts that are outlined here.

For those in theatre, there is a thrill every time the curtain goes up for an opening scene or comes down for a final curtain call. I still share my students' personal thrills, whether they have painted the throne on which Lear sits, or they are playing Lear himself. I hope you will experience the same thrill and pride when you say, "I did that."

—Roy A. Beck

Stagecraft

For many students, producing a play means *acting* in a play. In the total process of play production, however, acting happens to be just one part. A much larger "cast" is required offstage to effectively put on a play; scenery, lighting, sound effects, props, costumes, and make-up crews are just as important as acting in the play.

The cooperation of many people makes producing the play a highlight of a semester or school year. Dramas, musicals, or variety shows are traditions in many schools and colleges and should involve as many students as possible. Everyone should share in the thrill and enjoyment, as well as in the many tasks involved in producing the show. While the size of most play casts is limited, there are ample opportunities for your talents on the various crews whose task it is to build the scenery, run the lights, gather the props, or record the sound tape. The personal success of finding a place where you are accepted for your creative talents rather than for social or economic status is one of the biggest rewards of working in the theatre arts.

The Stage

The stage is any space where the action of a play can take place. Your school may have a complete auditorium, a raised platform at an end of the gym, a combination auditorium and cafeteria, or none at all. Stages, like people, come in all sizes and shapes.

Traditional Stage

The *traditional stage* is divided into three basic parts (see Fig. 1): the acting area, the apron, and the backstage area, which includes the wings to the right and left of the acting area. Usually these areas are enclosed in a frame called the proscenium arch, which frames the action of the play as a picture frame frames a picture. Many schools in this country have tended to limit their productions to the picture-frame concept. All of the action of the play takes place in the confines of the proscenium arch. In recent years, forward-thinking designers and directors in the theatre have tried to overcome this tendency by developing new concepts of staging. Arena staging and thrust or open staging are two examples of these new types.

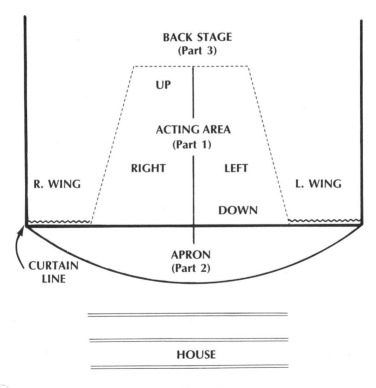

Fig. 1. Traditional stage.

Arena Stage

Arena staging was one of the first new concepts. In this type of staging, the actors occupy a center area, called the central acting area, and the audience is seated very close to the actors on all four sides of the arena (see Fig. 2). Some directors refer to arena staging as "acting in the round," for the audience surrounds the actors. Professor Glenn Hughes, in his book, *Penthouse Theatre*, illustrates how arena staging can be accomplished in varied situations. Flexibility is the prime advantage of arena staging; practically any interior setting can be staged arena style, or a modification of it. In a number of arena theatres, the seats are not permanently

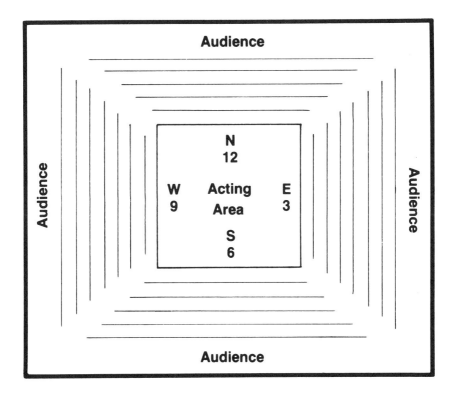

Fig. 2. Arena staging.

fixed or are put together in small rolling units, which permits staging the play along one side of the entire theatre or in just one corner of it. For instance, *The Queen and the Rebels* could be staged using just the upper left corner of the theatre for the setting, which could be built on eight-inch platforms to give the audience a better view of the actors. *Jacques Brel Is Alive and Well and Living in Paris* could be staged in arena style with the audience seated at sidewalk cafe tables.

Audiences in arena staging normally are kept small, 100 to 200 for each performance. The small audience offers a real advantage for budding thespians; it means more performances. Settings in the "round" should be kept to a minimum — usually just large props, such as tables, chairs, benches, etc. Care should be taken not to block the audience's view with tall scenery. It is typical that most plays currently produced in schools have interior settings, and these settings offer unlimited possibilities for arena staging. Nearly every school has an area that can be used for an arena stage; the cafeteria, large lobby, choral room, or perhaps the gym floor can be converted to an intimate arena stage with only a little creative imagination and work. Arena staging, even with added performances, offers one of the most economical methods of play production. The only limitation is the creative imagination of the group producing the play.

Open or Thrust Stage
The most recent development in staging is the *open* or *thrust stage* (see Fig. 3). Mr. James Hull Miller is credited with developing this concept in his design of the Western Springs Theatre at Western Springs, Illinois. In effect, the apron of the traditional stage is extended into the house. The audience is seated on three sides of the "thrust" stage and the acting area is moved forward so that most of the play's action takes place "down front." Settings usually are placed to the rear of the thrust, and some directors have effectively employed "projected" scenery by using a slide projector and painting the set design on the slides. Modifications of the thrust stage can be utilized in any school by building a stage extension of fifteen or twenty feet onto the apron.

Innovative and Creative Staging
Directors have always been innovative and creative in staging

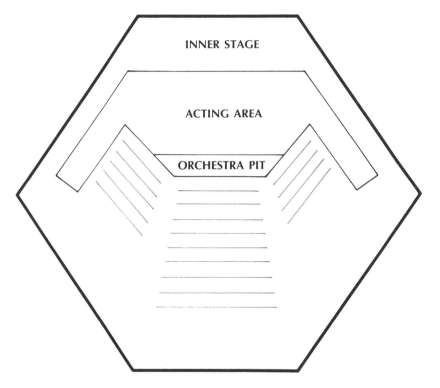

Fig. 3. Thrust stage.

plays. Faced with difficult financial problems, directors have staged plays in libraries and lunch rooms, and one group converted an old school coal bin into a fine arena theatre. Current trends in school budgeting tax the innovative powers of all who engage in and enjoy play production. In the history of the theatre, plays have been staged in nearly every conceivable space with a minimum of scenery and props. The purpose of the stage can be stated simply: to put life into action where all (the audience) can see it.

Stage Directions

In the drawing of the stage acting area in Fig. 1, all directions are given in terms of the actor as he or she faces the audience. "Up" is *away* from the audience; "down" is *toward* the audience. At one point in theatre history, the stage was built as an inclined plane sloping toward the audience, which was seated on a flat floor. Thus a move "up" meant a move up the incline and "down" meant to move down the incline. The great operatic composer, Richard Wagner, was one of the first to raise the audience on a sloped floor and to level out the stage. The terms "up" and "down," however, have remained a part of stage terminology.

Direction for arena stages (Fig. 2) are given in one of two ways: (1) according to the points of the compass or (2) according to the hands of the clock. Acting in and directing for arena stages calls for a great deal of adaptation on the part of both actors and directors. Directors may find that the hands of the clock are a little more precise in directing movements and placing settings in arena stages. For the open or thrust stage, directions are given the same way as for the traditional stage.

Scenery

Scenery is the environment or the locale of the play, created on the stage. As an environment, scenery should suggest to the audience where and when the play is taking place. Location (where) and time (when) are the two basic purposes for scenery on any stage or screen. How these two elements are achieved is determined by the stage, the equipment, and the talents of the scenic artist (see Fig. 4).

Scenery may be simple or very elaborate and still achieve the two basic purposes of location and time. Your stage may serve as a wrestling practice area, student meeting room, dance practice area, band practice area, and for countless other functions in addition to the speech and drama function for which it was intended. If scheduling the stage is a problem in your school, keep scenery simple! Overly ambitious and elaborate stage scenery, without adequate time or equipment to do a good job of it, is one of the biggest problems in school theatre. Also, economy of staging is wise from another perspective, the cost factor. For example, the cost of lumber and hardware used in creating stage sets has increased tremendously in the past several years. Good stage scenery does not have to be elaborate and naturalistic to create the environment necessary for the play. Scenery should contribute to the total presentation; it should not stand out in a lavish display of scenic wonderment. Likewise, it should not be so badly done

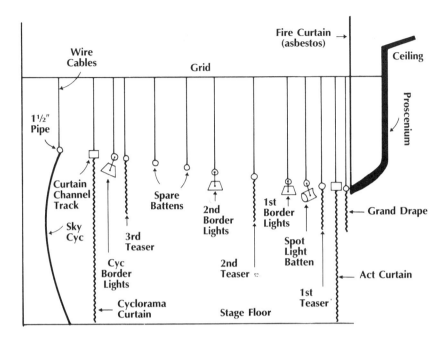

Fig. 4. Cross-section of a traditional stage.

that it detracts from the totality of the production. The old adage "In simplicity there is beauty" should be the rule for directors, scene designers and stage crews.

Methods of Staging

The action of most plays takes place either inside or outside; inside action is called *interior* and outside action is called *exterior*. Occasionally, plays have no specific setting, or have so many settings that making all of the sets would be an impossible task. Such settings are labeled *formal* or *space* settings. Many classical dramas from the Greek and Roman periods have this type of setting, as well as many Shakespearean plays (see Fig. 5). Thornton Wilder's *Our Town* is a modern adaptation of the Greek bare stage concept of staging. Locale and time in formal settings are usually indicated by costumes, program notation, and the language of the actors.

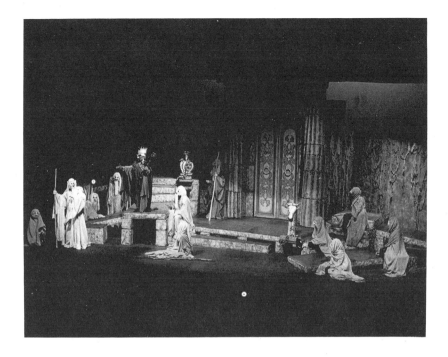

Fig. 5. Stylized setting for *Oedipus Rex*, Western Michigan University, Laura V. Shaw Theatre. Directed by Zack York, designed by Vern Stillwell.

Bare Stage
A bare stage with dramatic downshafts of light can be used for some types of plays, usually those not realistic in nature. Fantasies, dream plays, and psychodramas—in addition to the classical and Shakespearean plays—can be staged on a bare stage using minimum lighting and curtains.

Cyc Settings
Nearly every school stage has a set of cyclorama curtains. The cyclorama begins just inside the proscenium arch and surrounds the acting area (see Fig. 6). Usually the curtains are a neutral color: tan, gray, or beige. The word cyclorama means *surrounding* and is called a "cyc" by most people. Next to the bare stage method of staging, the cyc setting is the most economical. Cyc settings are quick to arrange and have been used by many schools

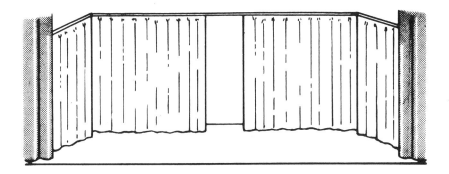

Fig. 6. Cyclorama curtains.

very effectively. By adding selected props such as tables, chairs, and couches, the set quickly resembles a living room. The number of plays set in living rooms is amazing. Almost any interior setting can be placed in the cyc set by using appropriately selected historical furniture and props. For those desiring a more realistic set, it is possible to add door and window units by inserting them between the individual curtains that make up the cyc. If your school's cyc is equipped with "headers" (short pieces of curtain between the longer curtains), it is possible to insert door and window units in them. It is a much neater looking arrangement than tying or pinning the longer cyc curtains around the doors and windows (see Fig. 7).

Exterior settings are occasionally needed, and they, too, can be placed in the cyc setting, especially if the stage is equipped

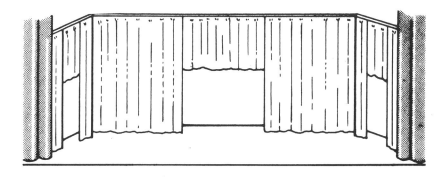

Fig. 7. Cyclorama curtains with headers.

with a sky cyc (either a light blue curtain hung behind the regular cyc up against the back wall, or the back wall of the stage itself is painted a light blue). Simple trees and "ground row" low foliage, plants, and flowers can be painted on Upson board (available from most lumber yards in 4′ × 8′ sheets) and cut out with a coping saw or trim knife (see Fig. 8). A cyc set can be used for plays that have more than one setting. Rapid changes can be made with cyc settings, and they are quite effective when properly used. It is interesting to note that when the musical *Oklahoma* opened on Broadway during World War II, nearly all of the exterior settings were of the simple cut-outs just described.

Set Pieces

A modification of the cyc setting is the "set piece" setting. Set pieces are key or important pieces of scenery that are required by the plot of the play. In the two-act drama, *The Staring Match*, by Jerry McNeely, it is necessary to have an old-fashioned well on the stage for the opening and the closing scenes. The well, constructed of 1″ × 3″ and Upson board, is placed on the stage for the opening scene, removed for most of the play, and returned for the final scene. This is a "set piece." Without it the plot of the play is not complete.

Fig. 8. Exterior set pieces.

The popular drama *The Curious Savage* requires a set of French doors and bookcases located up center. These pieces, plus entrances, are all that are really required, yet the stage is commonly filled with scenery for this play. Creative use of imagination can simplify the task of the stage setting and save the stage crew precious time and money.

Profile Sets

An extension of the set piece setting is the *profile set*. Profiles (see Fig. 9) are "suggested" full sets, but are seldom full height. Walls are suggested by laying flats on the long side rather than standing them upright, which makes a wall about five feet high. Doors and window units are placed, but there is no attempt to hide entrances or exits of actors (unless required by the plot) by surrounding them with flats or cyc curtains. Settings in profile can be as realistically or suggestively done as the director wishes. A door opening, for example, can be suggested with upright pieces of 1″ × 6″, and walls with pieces of Upson board stapled to

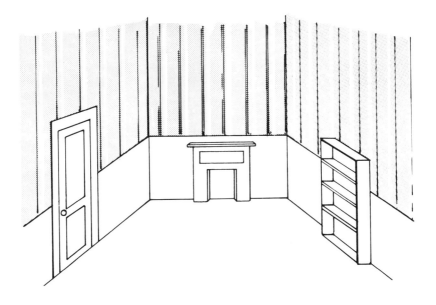

Fig. 9. Interior profile set.

a 1″ × 2″ frame, cut in an irregular shape to avoid too many parallel lines. Profiles should be high enough to be seen and recognized by the audience. A variety of heights adds visual interest. Because of the open nature of both arena and thrust stages, they are ideal for profile sets. Too much scenery height in either of these theatres can block the audience's view. Many interesting and exciting effects can be created with profile sets.

Full Set

A full set consists of stage scenery (flats) from the curtain line stage right to the curtain line stage left with little or no interruption. There are many variations and degrees of full settings. The typical full set is the *box set* (see Fig. 10). With a box set you attempt to enclose the acting area with a realistic room set, and all three walls are created with flats. In most schools the box set will be the first thing considered, after the play is selected. A full setting should be considered under the following four conditions:

Fig. 10 Full realistic setting for *Look Back in Anger*, Western Michigan University, Laura V. Shaw Theatre. Directed by Robert L. Smith, designed by Roy Beck.

1. There must be *adequate time* for building the set.

2. There must be *adequate space* for building, free from other school activities.

3. There must be *proper tools and equipment* available.

4. No other method of staging can be used effectively.

Regardless of the method of staging, it must be remembered that the available facilities, your talent as a scenic artist, and the time allotted for scenery construction determine the quality of the set for the play. Of these limiting conditions, time is most important. A good play setting cannot be produced in the three days before the play is to be presented, or even a week before. For this reason, a number of directors make out a production schedule by which each phase of the stagecraft must be completed. When rehearsals begin for the play, work should begin on the set.

Designing Scenery

The first step in planning scenery is to determine the type of staging that best suits the play selected. It has already been emphasized that methods more economical than full set should be considered very seriously. Scenery is usually the second most expensive item in most straight plays; the first is usually the royalty. In musicals, costuming is frequently the most expensive item. For many years, some school plays have been produced with poorly copied sets from the pictures and floor plans in the back of the play script. The sets pictured in the play script are usually from a Broadway production where cost was not an important factor, and they were designed for a stage far better equipped than most school stages. The obvious disadvantages are too much scenery for a very small stage, far too elaborate set decoration, and construction that can be done only by professional designers and carpenters. A final disadvantage is the lack of creativity. The hurried, harassed, overworked play director, who does not have time to properly create the scenery, should utilize the talents of students in this area of design (see the bibliography). What is intended here is a *practical* guide to designing scenery.

Step 1. Read the play at least twice before attempting to

design anything. A designer needs to be familiar with all aspects of the play. Nearly all plays require certain things, as prescribed by the playwright; i.e., doors, windows, levels, special pieces of furniture, or fixtures. The playwright describes the setting from experience and as it is visualized. During the second reading, make a list of what is *required* by the play. Note the locations suggested by the script and other possible locations that might be used.

Step 2. *Confer with the director.* Secure ideas and suggestions concerning the set design from the director. Every director has a mental picture of what the finished play set should look like. The reasons for selecting the play sometimes are based upon the ease of set construction. Most directors' theatrical experiences can be of invaluable aid to a designer. Make careful written notes of the suggestions.

Step 3. *Research the historical period of the play.* This activity is particularly useful for period plays, and is very helpful for some early twentieth-century plays. A play always takes place at a given time, and that specific time must be projected visually to the audience. With these preliminary data, the designer is ready to approach the stage on which the play set is to be built.

Step 4. *How much space is available?* Equipped with ruler, yardstick, or a 25- or 50-foot tape ruler, the designer takes the measurements. How much room does the set require? How much backstage room is there for bracing, passage for actors, prop storage, etc.? How much room do the actors need onstage? Will the proposed set aid the actor rather than hinder? These questions can be answered only by knowing the amount of space on the stage. Measure the stage from the act curtain to the back wall and from the edge of the act curtain right to the edge of the act curtain left, when the curtain is fully open. Then measure from the cyc curtain up right to the cyc curtain up left. It is a good idea to have a small drawing resembling the stage with you to record the exact measurements.

Step 5. *Determine the sightlines for your stage.* Sit in the front of the auditorium as far right as possible; then look at the stage. How much of the offstage area can you see? Look both right and left and especially note how much of the backstage area is exposed near the front curtain line. Next, move to the far left of the auditorium and repeat the procedure. If your stage is in the 'gym, you will need to set up a chair where the front row is usually placed for play performances. It might be wise to check with the person in charge of setting up the chairs. If your auditorium has a balcony, it must be checked as well, particularly from the front-row seat in the center, as you observe the approximate set height. Sight lines help you determine how much the act curtain must be closed after the set is constructed to hide or mask the backstage area. You may want to experiment with the sightlines by closing the curtain just a little and taking another look at the stage. Be sure to measure how far the curtain is closed. Once you have found the opening that seems to work best, mark it with two pieces of colored tape or masking tape. Put one piece of tape on each rope of the main curtain pull at eye level so they are easy to locate; the two marks should be parallel to each other. In this way, the exact opening can be repeated each time the curtain is opened.

Step 6. Make a floor plan of the set. With the dimensions from measurement of the stage and the sightlines, begin a rough floor plan of the set (see Fig. 11). Graph paper is suitable for the

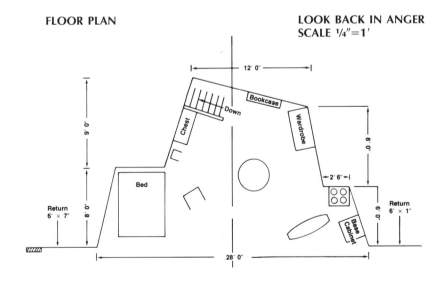

Fig. 11. *Look Back in Anger* floor plan.

first floor plan of the set. With the center line of the stage drawn on the graph paper, begin the placement of main entrances and exits, major set pieces, and large furniture props. Be sure to consult your notes from your conference with the director concerning the location of the doors and major set props. If there is a level change with platforms in the set, be sure to note the placement of the platform. Once these major items have been arranged, begin planning the placement of walls in terms of flats. If you have not already done so, now is a good time to check the existing flats the school has in storage. Indicate the size (width) of each flat on your rough floor plan. It is not unusual to make several rough floor plan drawings before you and the director agree on placement and arrangements.

Once the director agrees to a floor plan, it is wise to make an enlarged scale drawing of the plan, with one-half inch equaling one foot. Check once again with the director when the enlarged scale drawing is complete. If the director agrees, begin "taping the set" on the stage floor. Using ¾″ or 1″ masking tape, lay out the entire set just as you have drawn it. Leave doorways blank and indicate windows by putting a short piece of tape across the wall line. In some school situations, taping may not be possible because of conflicting activities. In such cases, you will need to draw the set lines with chalk—a number of times. With the set taped or chalked on the stage, the actors will know where they can and cannot move during rehearsals.

Step 7. *Make a rough perspective sketch of the set.* A rough sketch of the set is not difficult to execute; you do not have to be an artist to make this working sketch. Begin with a line indicating the center of the stage and construct a box around the center line representing the stage house. On the back and sides of the box you can detail parts of the set. If you have some art ability you know that the parts must be in proportion, the front details larger than those in the back. Should you encounter difficulty you may want to check with the art instructor or a friend who is good at drawing for help. Once you have the perspective sketch drawn, it is wise to check with the director to see if what you have drawn is what the director had in mind. You can color the perspective with pastels, water color, or tempera. This is a good time to experiment with various color combinations for the setting.

Step 8. *Make a model of the set.* Making a set model is an activity that many students enjoy. Using the floor plan and the rough sketch you have made, begin your model set by making flats of heavy cardboard, using the ½" equals 1' scale. Make each flat individually, just as you plan to do it on the stage. Light-weight cardboard or illustration board is excellent for this purpose. Once you have cut out with a razor blade or knife the flats to be used, paint them (with water colors or tempera) the color you and the director have selected for the set. The model should be decorated the way you intend to decorate the finished set. Plastic doll furniture can be used to furnish the set, but it is possible to make the furniture from cardboard or balsa wood. During the model construction you will encounter problems much like those in building the real set.

LOOK BACK IN ANGER: Description of Flats

Stage Right	Size	Special	Paint
1. Return	6' × 7'		black, gray base,
2. R-1	4' × 7'	casement window	etc.
3. R-2	4' × 7'	2' × 2',	
4. R-3	5' × 7'	4" up/bottom	
5. R-4	4'6" × 7'		
6. R-5	4'6" × 7'		
7. R-6	6' × 7'		

Stage Left	Size		Paint
1. Return	6' × 14'		black,
2. L-1	6' × 14'		gray base,
3. L-2	2'6" × 14'		spatter dk. brown,
4. L-3	4' × 14'		olive, black
5. L-4	4' × 14'		
6. L-5	6' × 7'		

Special
SR-1 triangle 3' × 6' (fits atop R-6)
SL-2   3' and 7' stiles × 6' bottom rail
        (fits atop L-5)

SL-2 has casement type windows 1' up from bottom rail and is full 6' wide 2' high.

SET WILL SPLIT AT L-5 and R-6. Left side to be stored behind blacks at the rear left. Right side to be stored behind blacks at the rear right.

Fig. 12. Flat list for *Look Back in Anger*.

It should be noted that not all designers follow all of the steps outlined here. Many excellent professional designers have never worked from a model; others have never made a rough perspective. If you are seriously interested in scene design, futher study of books on scene design and as much practice as you can get is recommended.

Figure 12 is a description of the flats selected from permanent stock and units to be constructed (under "Special") for *Look Back in Anger*. Once the design has been approved by the director, the flats and scenery units to make the setting need to be selected. Full set walls can be put together in a number of different ways using various sizes of flats. Stability and ease of handling, particularly if there are scene shifts involved, should determine which flats are selected to make up the set walls. Trying various combinations on the stage can sometimes aid in the selection. Once the flats are selected each should be lettered *L* for left and *R* for right, with notes on the individual flat repairs, color, and special treatment. Such a chart is of great value to the stage crew in getting the set ready and up for the show.

Arena Scenery

Plays staged in arena style normally do not require scenery as extensive as that used on the traditional stage. When plays are produced in the full round, they usually require only furniture or property setting. When a modified arena is used, either three-sided or half round, low pieces of scenery can be used. Screen settings in arena staging should be used because the audience usually is very close to the play's action. If the audience is close, a good deal of attention should be given to construction detail to ensure well-made sets.

The designing of sets for the arena follows the same basic steps outlined for the traditional stage, but the designer should note that what is acceptable for an audience in proscenium staging may not be acceptable in arena. Extreme artificiality, unless it is a part of the play, will not be accepted by most audiences because they are so much a part of the play. Designs for arena settings should consider: (1) the minimum essential set pieces, (2) entrance and exit of actors, and (3) utilization of the playing space.

Composite settings in arena designs fuse all parts or places into a single set within the playing space (see Fig. 13). Certain areas of the space can be designated as the living room, dining room, and courtyard. These areas usually overlap in the center of the playing space. *Single sets*, as in the traditional stage, represent a specific locale, usually a room, and the decoration must convey to the audience the element of time. The placement of furniture is very important, since it should not block the action of the play and the action should be visible to most of the audience.

In any form of arena staging, it is imperative that the director and the designer work together.

Making Scenery

The people in most schools who can help the stage crew beyond measure in building scenery are the custodial staff and the industrial arts instructors. These people have many duties to perform, and it is a *wise* stage crew that tactfully approaches them early in the stages of play production and asks for their assistance.

Fig. 13. Composite set for *Purlie Victorious* by Western Michigan's Arena Theatre. Directed by Robert L. Smith.

If the school does not have a scene shop as a part of its stage facilities, the next area of the school properly equipped for making scenery is the industrial arts department. Making scenery calls for precision cutting of materials, and this can best be accomplished with power equipment. If tactfully approached, most industrial arts teachers are willing to help stage crews cut out and, in some cases, assemble scenery. This does not mean that the responsibility for building the scenery is given to the industrial arts teacher; building scenery is the responsibility of the scenery crew. Should members of the stage crew know how to handle power equipment (such knowledge usually comes from an industrial arts course in woodworking), the request may be to use the school's equipment in building the scenery. If your school is fortunate enough to have a scene shop with power equipment, it is important that only members of the crew who know how to handle power equipment do so. Power saws, particularly, are dangerous in the hands of people who do not know how to use them.

Custodians are familiar with the places stage crews can find the things—in and out of the school—that are needed to build scenery, and local sources of supply are valuable to any stage crew. Using the stage for scenery building also presents problems for the custodian, unless consulted before the crew begins work. Custodians are among the most valuable "friends" any play-producing group can have. Needless to say, these individuals should be given program credit for their help in producing the play. Having consulted both the industrial arts instructor and the custodian, the scenery crew is ready to go to work.

Basic Flat and Screen Construction

A "flat" consists of a wooden frame covered with muslin or canvas; it is usually from 10' to 16' in height. A "screen" differs only in height; it is from 6' to 9' high. Stage scenery, in general, is not constructed with permanence in mind, although flats and screens usually last from three to five years, or even longer, depending upon care and use. Scenery is not built "solid as a rock," as one would build a home or a shop project. Scenery should be light-weight, easily moved, and adaptable to a variety of situations. A flat resembles an artist's canvas; indeed, the historical origin of flats was in Renaissance Italy, where some of the great artists were employed for scenic painting.

Flat sizes, particularly their height, depend upon the height of the proscenium opening and whether or not the curtain borders are adjustable up and down. Very tall flats on a small stage tend to give the illusion of a very high ceiling. Further, they tend to give an air of formality to whatever play is done. In most school situations, 10' to 12' flats give a much more intimate feeling, a desirable characteristic for most modern plays. Flat widths are more historical than practical. Flats were made 5' to 9' wide simply because that was the size of the door opening on old railway cars and also the size of the stage door. Practically speaking, a flat can be *any* width, according to its purpose. Figure 14 lists a so-called "stock" set of flats, usable for many plays and stage purposes. If your school does not have a set of flats, it is best to begin with these stock sizes. Since flats will need to be used from play to play and year to year, it is important that they be a *standard* size. Flats wider than 5'9" are difficult to handle and to store on the stage.

Screens are recommended for schools with minimum stage facilities and a small stage area. Screens have the advantage over regular flats in that they are lighter in weight and more easily moved. Screens work better as set pieces and in profile sets than do regular flats. Most plays produced in high schools usually do not require extreme "realistic" or "naturalistic" settings but rather require only an illusion on the stage. Screens fulfill this requirement very effectively. In making a flat or screen: (1) select the lumber; (2) cut the lumber; (3) assemble the flat or screen; and (4) cover the flat or screen.

Selecting the Lumber

Selecting lumber for the construction of flats or screens is an important task. The first decision is whether the flat or screen is to be used only for one play, or added to the permanent stock of scenery. Permanent flats are usually constructed with better grades of lumber than temporary scenery. Temporary, or one-show, flats can be made from several common grades of lumber. Firring strips (1" × 2"), used in the home to panel walls, can be used, as well as common grades of 1" × 3" and 1" × 4". Lumber is classified today as "common" and "Upper." Upper is better than common. Within each classification are several grades; upper

Standard Size Flats		Recommended Screen Sizes	
	Recommended		
Width	Height	Width	Height
5'9"	10' – 12'	5'0"	8' – 9'
4'0"	10' – 12'	4'0"	8' – 9'
3'6"	10' – 12'	3'0"	8' – 9'
3'0"	10' – 12'	2'0"	8' – 9'
2'6"	10' – 12'	1'0"	8' – 9'
2'0"	10' – 12'		
1'0"	10' – 12'		

Fig. 14. Standard flats and screens.

grades are B and Better, C, and D. Common grades are 2, 3, and 4. Nationally, the dimensions of lumber have changed in order to conserve lumber which is growing short in supply. What is called 1″ × 3″ in this text, and by most lumberyards, has actual dimensions of ¾″ × 2½″; a 2″ × 4″ actually measures 1½″ × 3½″. Lumber people still use the *full inch* dimensions when referring to lumber stock.

Flats to be added to the permanent stock of scenery should be constructed from the upper grades of lumber, which are generally clearer, have fewer knots and less warp. A permanent flat, properly constructed, can serve for years and be remodeled several times for other plays. White pine is preferred to other woods because of its durability, close grain, and ease of working. If white pine is not available, or the cost is prohibitive in your area, fir is the next best choice. Two by fours are generally available in fir rather than pine. Fir does have a tendency to split and splinter rather easily.

Learning to select lumber is an experience stage crew members should have, and for this reason it is strongly recommended that they personally visit the lumber company to help select the lumber for the play. The personnel of most lumber yards have a great deal of knowledge about wood and its use that is invaluable to a stage crew member. Lumber should be inspected to make certain all pieces will meet the needs of the set to be built — even the "common" grades vary considerably in knots and warp.

Selection should be made to get stock as straight as possible. Knots can frequently be worked around in the cutting process. If lumber is ordered by phone, the grade, thickness, width (in full inches), and length should be stated. It is also wise to inquire about the cost, since lumber prices are usually on the increase. Waste should be kept to a bare minimum, but crews and directors are apt to make mistakes in figuring, cutting, or laying out the scenery. Therefore, it is wise to order more than is absolutely essential to build the necessary units. Ordering stock in longer lengths (12' and 16') assures a sufficient supply of lumber on hand when needed. Lumber companies figure lumber in *board feet*, whereas most flats are figured in *lineal feet* or meters. To avoid the board feet-lineal feet confusion, it is best to order lumber by the number of lengths (12' or 16') needed. For example: a single 5' × 10' flat requires four (4) 12' lengths, with about 4'6" left over for a toggle bar on another flat.

Cutting the Lumber

Figure 15 represents the parts of a flat. The top and bottom are called *rails*; the side pieces are called *stiles*; the center brace is called a *toggle bar*. Each flat or screen consists of five pieces:

> 2 rails—cut the exact width of the finished flat or screen.
>
> 2 stiles—cut 2 times the width of the stock *less* than the finished height of the flat or screen.
>
> 1 toggle bar—cut 2 times the width of the stock *less* than the finished width of the flat.

A square should be used to mark all cuts, even when using power saws with cross-cut gauges and guides. Before making any cuts it is wise to check and *double check* all measurements. Always allow 1/16" for saw cuts. Once the rails, stiles, and toggle bar have been cut, the assembly involves the following steps: (1) squaring the corners, (2) attaching the corner blocks, and (3) attaching the keystones.

Squaring the corners was, for a number of years, one of the major problems scenery crews had in making flats. Today, thanks to a picture-frame miter clamp, *any* scenery crew can build square flats. Picture-frame miter clamps can be purchased at nearly all hardware stores for a reasonable price. Make certain the clamps

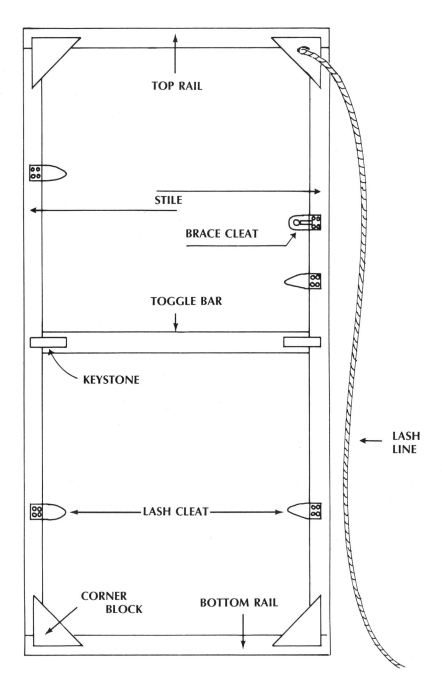

Fig. 15. Parts of a flat.

will open to 3″, because they come in various sizes. The crew hard-pressed for cash can operate with one set, although two sets are recommended for assembly-line building. The picture-frame miter clamps are attached to the top rail and stiles by sliding the 1″ × 3″ into the clamp opening and screwing it tight. Make certain the rail and stile touch at each corner. Frequently, saw cuts will be uneven; so let the clamp square the corner! Do not force two unevenly cut pieces of wood together. The clamps should not be removed until the corner blocks have been attached.

Corner blocks are made from ¼″ plywood cut in an 8½″ × 6″ triangle (see Fig. 16). The grain on the top layer of plywood should run as illustrated for maximum support. If the grain runs counter to this, there is danger that the block will crack, as the top layers of plywood are stronger than the inner core.

Cutting corner blocks from plywood calls for a practical application of geometry, and perhaps a few hints on handling the plywood would not spoil the problem of how to cut the triangles. Begin by ripping the plywood sheet (4′ × 8′) in half (2′ × 4′). This makes it much easier to handle and does not affect the number of corner blocks and keystones one is able to cut out of a sheet.

There are several methods of attaching corner blocks to the flat frame. Nailing is the first method, using either clout nails or blue lath nails. A *clout nail* is a special soft metal, flat-sided nail, designed to curl under when it strikes a hard surface, steel, or

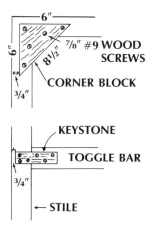

Fig. 16. Corner block and keystone.

concrete. The clout nail forms a very secure bond between the corner block and the flat frame. Clout nails (1¼″) are a special kind of hardware available *only* from theatre supply houses. Blue lath nails (1″ or 1¼″) are a substitute for clout nails because they are readily available from lumberyards and hardware stores. The 1″ lath nail usually does not need to be clinched (bent over on the front side of the flat); however the 1¼″ does need to be clinched. When corner block or keystone nails are clinched on the front side of the flat, it is important that they be buried in the wood so that no sharp points are sticking up at any point or they may tear the muslin or canvas covering of the flat when it is sized. A good grade of white glue is usually applied to the down side of the corner block before it is nailed. Be certain to keep both the corner block and keystones ¾″ from the outside edge of the stile of the flat. It helps to keep a scrap of 1″ × 3″ to use as a template guide for this measurement.

Attaching corner blocks and keystones with screws is another method of assembly. Five holes need to be drilled through the block and part way into the stile and rail. Use a ⅛″ bit in either an electric drill or hand-type push drill; this is just about the right size to take the #9, ⅞″ wood screws used to attach the block. The drilling pattern seen in Fig. 16 gives strength to the joint. Once all four corners have been attached, the toggle bar is fitted in the center of the wooden frame and attached to the right and left stiles with keystones. Keystones are ¼″ pieces of plywood, about 5″ or 6″ long and 2½″ or 3″ wide, and are attached to the toggle bar and rail with five screws, as are the corner blocks. It is not necessary to use the picture-frame miter clamps on these joints. To test the squareness of the flat, stand it on all four sides; it should stand straight on each side.

Covering the Flat

Covering the flat involves the following steps: (1) laying on the unbleached muslin, (2) gluing and stapling the muslin, and (3) trimming the muslin.

Unbleached muslin is the least expensive and most readily available covering material for flats or screens. Most dry goods and department stores handle unbleached muslin in 36″ and 48″ widths. While these widths are usually too narrow for 5′ flats or screens, they work nicely for narrower flats. Scenic muslin, slightly heavier, comes in 72″ and 78″ widths and is much easier to work. Scenic muslin is cheaper when purchased in bolts of 50 to 70 yards, but it can be bought by the yard from some theatrical supply houses. Any group planning to build a new stock of flats or add a considerable number to its present stock should consider purchasing muslin in bolts rather than by the yard. Several large textile mills run specials on muslin at least once a year, and a school can realize a considerable saving by purchasing at these times. Narrower widths can, in an emergency, be sewed together. A seam will appear in the middle, but this is usually not too noticeable once the flat is painted, provided the seam has been closely stitched. The prime disadvantage in sewing muslin together is that the seam is the first place the flat will come apart. While some scenery makers advocate using canvas, it is not recommended. Canvas is bulky and difficult to work with. In addition, the cost is about twice that of unbleached muslin.

Using 72″ muslin, unroll enough so that about 6″ extend over the bottom and top rails and the left and right stiles. The flat frame should be lying face up on the stage or scene-shop floor. Face up means that the corner blocks and keystones will be resting on the floor. The muslin *should not be pulled tight* but should lie loosely on the frame and slightly off the floor. If muslin is stretched too tightly before it is sized or painted, it can warp and twist the entire flat out of shape. A tack or staple should be placed in each of the four corners to hold the muslin in place.

Gluing the muslin to the frame is the next step. Three kinds of glue may be used for this purpose: any of the white glues on the market today, Elmer's or Leech glue (frequently used by art departments), or casein glue. Be certain to spread the glue on *both* sides of the muslin to be glued to the rails and stiles. Mix the casein glue with water (warm or cold) and spread it on the muslin and wood with a paint brush. Another type of glue is regular hide glue, which must be prepared in a double boiler or a glue pot. The bonding power of hide glue is greater than either the white or casein glues, but it involves more preparation (soaking and heating) and has a rather unpleasant odor.

The glue is spread along the stile first; then the muslin is pressed down on it and another application of glue is put on the muslin. A piece of scrap lumber about 3″ long will help smooth out the wrinkles. *Be careful not to stretch the muslin or pull it too tightly*. Glue the entire flat first; then staple or tack. The reason for this is to avoid developing wrinkles in the muslin which could show up later. Glue the rails in the same manner as the stiles, making certain the wrinkles are smoothed out completely by pulling the muslin toward the outer edges of the rails. Finally, a row of tacks or staples about 6″ apart is placed all around the frame, rails, and stiles. *Never glue or tack the toggle bar; let it alone!* It is best to allow eight to twelve hours for the glue to dry properly; so it is advised that all gluing and stapling of muslin be done in one work session. Once the muslin on the rails and stiles has dried, the surplus muslin must be trimmed off ¼″ to ½″ in from the outer edge of the flat with a trim knife or single-edge razor blade (see Fig. 17). Make the first cut on the stile and gently pull the surplus as you cut, in order to keep the material taut and make the cutting easier. The pull-cutting operation takes a little practice to get the right amount of tension, but it makes a neatly finished flat. The flats are now ready for the final preparation step, sizing.

Sizing is the process of filling the weave of the muslin fibre with a glue and water mixture to make painting easier. Sizing also

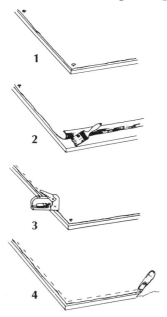

Fig. 17. Gluing, stapling, and trimming.

shrinks the muslin a great deal and makes the flat tight, like an artist's canvas. Flats that have not been sized before painting may warp, and the paint, when applied, will "bleed" through the open weave.

Size water is a mixture of glue and water. The mix is made as follows: one cup of hide glue to one gallon of water. Commercial wall sizing, available in most paint stores, will work *if it is thinned* with more water after the directions on the package have been followed. If it is applied according to directions, it is too heavy with glue and the muslin becomes hard and brittle. Add water a little at a time to the commercial wall sizing until your fingers just stick together. Brush sizing on just as though you were painting the flat. The stage floor, if that is where the painting is to be done, should be protected with a layer of old newspapers or plastic dropcloths. Sized flats should stand for twenty-four hours before applying the base coat of paint.

Door and Window Flats

Door (see Fig. 18) and window flats are modifications of the basic flat-construction process. Door and window flats are usually 5'9" in width, and seldom less than 5'6". The reason for this is so the door flat or window flat, when used alone as a set piece, does not appear out of proportion.

The major parts of a 5'9" door flat are as follows:

2 outer stiles	2 inner stiles
1 top rail	2 short toggle bars
1 toggle bar	6 corner blocks, 4 keystones
2 bottom rails	

The top rail and the two outer stiles are assembled as in the basic flat. The long toggle bar is placed so it is exactly 3' from the top of the top rail to the bottom of the toggle bar. Inner stiles and bottom rails can be assembled as separate units, using the picture-frame miter clamps at all corners. Remember, the stile rests on the rail. The assembled inner stiles are laid in the assembled outer frame. The corner blocks used on the inner stiles need to be trimmed on one corner so they will fit properly without overlapping. Remember to keep the corner blocks ¾" from the outer

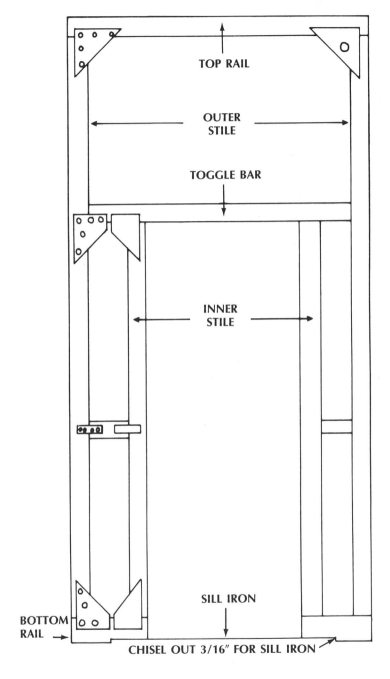

Fig. 18. Door flat.

edge of the flat. Corner blocks should be trimmed before they are attached to the flat frame. Note that corner blocks are used on the inside, where the inner stile and the toggle bar meet; this is for added strength. Be certain to follow the drill-hole pattern for attaching all corner blocks.

To cover door flats, use three pieces of muslin. Lap them on the long toggle bar and use a single row of staples or tacks to ensure that the muslin will not pull loose. After the muslin has been applied and trimmed, as in the basic flat, a "saddle iron" is added to the bottom of the frame. Saddle irons, or "sill irons," can be purchased from commercial theatrical supply companies (be sure to give the exact size of the opening). Saddle irons can be made from $\frac{3}{16}'' \times \frac{3}{4}''$ strap iron that is cut 6″ shorter than the bottom rails. A sill iron of some nature is necessary to give stability to all door flats.

Window flats are constructed just as the door flat and basic flat, with the following exceptions: (1) the bottom rail is complete — 5′9″; (2) the sill of the window is placed 3′ up from the bottom rail; (3) the opening for the window should be 3′ × 4′. Assembly of the window flat is the same as for the basic flat or door flat. Extra toggle braces usually are added to window flats at the 5′ mark. A window flat can be covered with one piece or with four pieces of muslin, lapping at the bottom and top toggle bars.

It is possible to convert door flats into window flats by using a 3′ × 3′ plug, made of Upson board, and a wooden frame. The plug should be nailed or screwed to the inner stiles of the door flat, and a "dutchman" is used to cover the cracks. A dutchman is a 5″ or 6″ strip of muslin that is applied to the flat with paint to hide cracks, such as those made by the plug.

Stndardization of door and window flat is not a necessity since the scenery needs will vary from play to play, and many sizes may be used to fit any situation. What has been described here are stock sizes.

Door Frames and Window Frames

The door and window flats just described are not complete and ready to place on the stage. A frame to hold the door and windows is necessary for them to be functional. The door frame (see Fig. 19) is constructed as follows:

Two 1″ × 6″ × 6′6″
Two 1″ × 6″ × 6′10″
One 1″ × 6″ × 2′10″
One 1″ × 6″ × 3′

The door frame is made to be slid in the flat, from the front, so the frame facing rests against the flat. The jamb of the door is the depth the door goes into the flat. The jamb of the door is built by using the two 6′6″ pieces and the two 2′10″ pieces of 1″ × 6″. The frame should measure 6′6″ *inside*, not outside. Place the 3′ piece

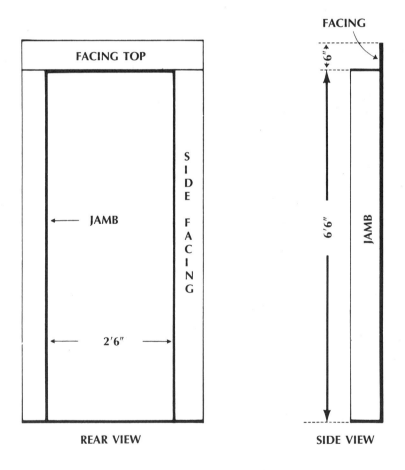

Fig. 19. Door frame.

so it rests on top of the two long 1" × 6"s. Use either flat L's or mending plates to join the pieces together. The jamb is assembled by using 1½" #9 wood screws and 90° L's (see Fig. 20). The jamb is now laid on the floor and the facing frame is laid on top of it. The two units are joined in a butt joint with 1½" #9 wood screws in at least six places on the facing frame. The facing frame will be fragile, so handle it carefully when placing it on the jamb. Once the wood screws are countersunk securely, the unit can be turned over on the facing and more 90° L's are added to hold the two units together firmly. Be careful not to use too many L's on the top, as they might block the easy sliding of the door frame into the door flat.

The bottom sill should be beveled with a draw knife or a plane to prevent actors from stumbling over the sill. The door which is attached to the frame is made the same size as the *inside* dimensions of the frame. The door is made of either Upson board or

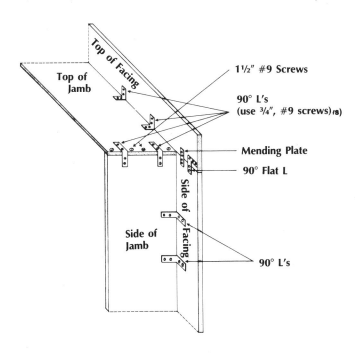

Fig. 20. Door frame assembly detail.

plywood. Upson board is preferable since it is lighter and easier to work, and it is cheaper. The door can be as plain or ornate as desired. It is best to begin with a plain door and decorate it as needed with picture frame mouldings of various widths and thicknesses. Rope has been used to create Victorian ornate doors, and thin strips of scrap lumber create interesting depth to doors. The door, without the Upson board cover, is built just as the flat frame was constructed; i.e., top rail and bottom rail are the exact same width and the stiles are shorter than the finished height. The Upson board is then tacked or stapled to the door. The door is hinged to the door frame with loose pin hinges on the *left side* for door frames going on stage right and on the *right side* for frames going on stage left. *Doors should always open* downstage (to mask the actors' entrance); *doors should be hinged* on the upstage side.

Window frames are constructed in a fashion similar to the door frame, except they are made shorter to fit the window flat. The width of the unit is the same. The height is 3'8" *inside* the window proper. While some designers make windows that slide up and down, like regular home windows, the author has found that small windowpanes can be designed and nailed to the jamb of the window as need dictates. Regular plaster lath or trellis material may be used to effect a variety of designs from modern to colonial windows. Door or window frames may be held in the flat by several methods. An old-fashioned 6" strap hinge can be placed at an angle on both sides of the jamb so that when it is opened it presses firmly against the flat stile. This method makes shifting the scenery very easy. Another method is to use either 1" × 3" or 2" × 4" blocks, 6" to 8" long, and screw them to the jamb once the frame is in the flat. This method is more permanent and is recommended for single-set plays only. Some stage crews use 90° L's to fasten the frame to the flat. Door and window flats should be braced with stage braces on both sides of the frame. Door frames in flats add considerable weight, and it is necessary to make certain they do not fall. It is not advised to use regular house doors for stage purposes; they are much too heavy and create more problems than they solve.

Platforms

Creating various levels on the stage is one of the most interesting effects a stage crew can produce. Platforms vary in height from 4″ to several feet. In the smaller heights, 4″ and 6″, it is best to build a solid platform using 2″ × 4″s or 2″ × 6″s for the outer frame and the "stringer" support. The author recommends that all platforms be built of a sheet of ¾″ A/D (A/D means one side good, the other side rough) plywood which is 4′ × 8′. If platforms are constructed in widths 4′ × 8′ and 2′ × 4′, it is possible to use one top for several platforms. (Sometimes the movable tops are called "lids".) The tops will interchange with the parallel platforms as well.

Tops or lids, made from ¾″ plywood and blocks, are placed on the rough side to prevent the lid shifting once it is on the platform. Tops should be padded with old carpeting, wrong side up, or with layers of newspaper and unbleached muslin. Avoid using any "noisy" substance as a covering material for lids.

Parallel platforms usually are constructed in 12″, 18″, 24″, 30″, and 36″ heights. The design of each is the same, and the leg heights and the braces just increase in size. In Fig. 21 the side and end structures are pictured. It is best to join the parallel with more than five screws at the joints. Remember, this structure is designed to give strength without weight. It is constructed of a 1″ × 3″ of the same quality used in building flats. In Fig. 22 the hinging process is illustrated. If this is not followed exactly, the parallel will not fold properly. Drop-pin hinges should be used.

There is a tendency for beginners to build platforms rock-solid with regular construction materials, the 2″ × 4″s, 2″ × 6″s, and 2′

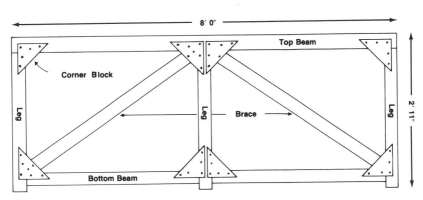

Fig. 21. Sides of the parallel platform.

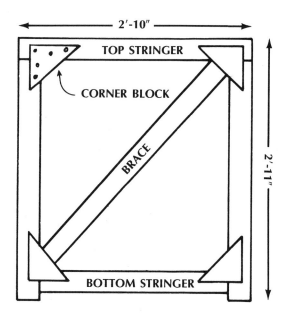

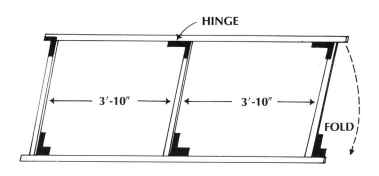

Fig. 22. The hinging process. *Above,* the ends and middle of the parallel platform. *Below,* placement of hinges.

× 8's used in home building. If you have ample storage space backstage, this is not a bad practice, as platforms to hold human beings *should* be strong. However, space limitations and costs should lead stage crews to consider building with lighter materials but constructing so as to gain maximum strength. While parallels of 1″ × 3″ or 1″ × 4″ are strong up to a height of three feet, platforms over that height must be built of 2″ × 4″ or 2″ × 6″ for sufficient strength and rigidity.

Special Sizes and Shapes

Any size or shape flat, door flat, door frame, or platform can be constructed to meet special needs. What has been described here are *basic* scenery construction methods and suggestions toward standardization in sizes. Most of the plays to be produced in schools today are one-set shows requiring such standard items.

Once the scenery is constructed it is ready for painting.

Fig. 23. Applying the base coat.

Painting

Just as the custodian and the industrial arts instructor were consulted in building scenery, the art instructor should be consulted about painting the set. The design, color, and texture are specialized areas of art, and it is quite likely that the painting crew will not have this specialized kind of knowledge. It is also possible that the director of the play will not have an extensive art education. Of course, do not hand over the responsibility of painting the set to the art instructor, merely ask for advice.

Painting scenery involves the following steps: (1) selecting the color or colors of the set, (2) mixing the base coat, (3) applying the base coat, and (4) texture coats.

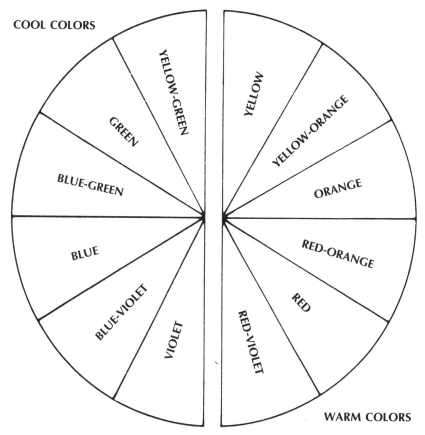

Fig. 24. Color wheel.

Color

Color is divided into two categories—warm and cool. Warm colors are best suited for comedies, farces, and plays that are not tragic in nature. Cool colors are best suited for serious dramas, mysteries, and classical plays. The color wheel (Fig. 24) illustrates the spectrum of warm and cool colors.

The theme of the play should determine the color of the scenery because certain colors denote certain attitudes and feelings.

Yellow: Cheerfulness, gaiety, lightheartedness, sunniness. If grayed, it indicates sickness, cowardice, jealousy.

Red: Violence, excitement, rage, danger, wrath, strife. Too much red area on the stage tires an audience quickly.

Green: Restful, youth, growth, faith. It is rather neutral in emotional impact unless it is very intense or blackened.

Purple: Royalty, nobility, death, sadness, and strength of spirit.

Blue: Coolness, serenity, vastness (of distance), aristocratic, nothingness.

Black: Gloom, death, depression. Too much black on the stage can depress an audience, but black, when mixed with other colors, can project degrees of gaiety, excitement, coolness, etc.

White: Truth, innocence, purity, chastity. White mixed with other colors also can project degrees of attitude or feeling.

Gray: Humility, resignation, old age.

Brown: Earthiness, commonness, poverty, oldness.

It is not possible to present all information concerning color here; however, this little bit of information should stimulate further research into the fascinating study of color. There should be many books on this subject in your library.

For many years all scenery was painted with regular artists' dry colors. Indeed, they are still used by many scenic artists. Frequently, scenery or paint crews have a great deal of difficulty in mixing dry paint properly. Therefore, a substitute of suitable quality is desirable.

Most major paint companies produce a waterbase *casein paint* that can be mixed in almost as many shades as dry color. Mixing casein paints is much simpler than mixing dry paints. Casein comes in a very thick consistency (much like butter), and mixing the gallon of base with a gallon and a half of water produces paint of about the thickness of heavy cream, just the right painting consistency. With casein paints, no glue need be added to the mix. If you use white as the base for nearly all colors, it will be possible to get the exact color desired, and white is rather in-expensive compared to the intense colors of raw umber and burnt sienna. As in dry color, a little intense color goes a long way; so add color slowly.

Casein paints are readily available from hardware and paint stores and from lumberyards. Scenery or paint crews can mix paint easily with minimum supervision by the director once the color and proper proportions have been determined. Mixing requires three or more 10-quart plastic buckets, a strong paint paddle, warm water, the base color, and tinting colors. A plastic measuring cup (one cup or one quart) will help in determining exact measurements. In the beginning, it is wise to mix more paint than you feel you will need. Casein paints keep for a week or more if they are covered with a wet towel or rag when not in use.

Applying the Base Coat

To apply the base coat of paint, all the flats are laid face up on the stage or the scene-shop floor. One should be certain that a walk space is left between the flats so that painters can walk all the way around a flat. Using 4″ — or better still, 6″ — nylon-bristle brushes, apply the paint by dipping the brush into the paint and wiping the excess off on the inside edge of the paint pail. Care should be taken not to get too much paint on the brush or to dip the brush too deeply in the paint. The paint is applied to the flat in a series of overlapping strokes, in the shape of figure 8s or Xs (see Fig. 23). Do not attempt to paint too far with one brushload of paint; dip the brush frequently in the paint.

Painting flats as they lie flat on the floor presents the possibility of puddling — of paint collecting in puddles at various points on the flat, usually near the center above and below the toggle bar. It is best to apply the base coat as you work from the center to the outer rail. Paint applied in figure 8s gives a much better texture than that applied in straight lines. The base coat should be allowed

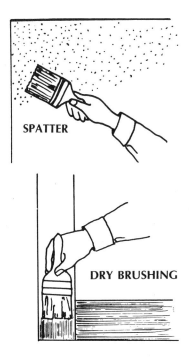

Fig. 25. Spattering and dry brushing.

to dry at least twelve hours before any other paint is applied to the flat.

It is best to stir the paint frequently, although casein paint settles out less than dry-color mixes. If many flats are to be painted, begin painting the flats at one end of the stage and work to the other end; in an hour or two the flats that were painted first have "set" enough that they can be leaned against the back wall of the stage and will take up much less space than if they were left lying flat.

Flats painted with a base coat are *not* complete; they lack texture and depth. To achieve both texture and depth, the flats need another paint treatment. Various methods have been employed by scenic artists to get the proper texture desired; spattering, dry-brushing, and spraying are examples.

Spattering

Spattering is one of the time-honored techniques. The brush, having been cleaned in water after applying the base coat, is dipped lightly into the paint color selected as the *first* spatter coat, and the paint is "flipped" toward the flat so that the paint lands in tiny drops. The brush can be struck against a board or hit against the hand. The size of the drops will vary with the amount of paint used — but be careful not to get too much paint; this will spoil the entire effect. It is suggested that a practice flat be used for developing the spattering technique.

The color of the first spatter coat should be either a full shade lighter or darker than the base coat but of the same hue. A good rule of thumb is that if the base coat is light, spatter with a darker shade first; if the base coat is dark, spatter with a lighter shade first. The second spatter coat can be applied once the first coat has had time to dry, usually in three or four hours. The second coat should be of an opposite color — across the color wheel from the base color (see fig. 24). Care should be taken not to spatter opposite colors too heavily, as they will "turn" the color of the set very quickly. A third and fourth spatter coat can be applied, depending upon the texture desired. To make flats look old, spatter them with dark brown and black, especially near the top of the flat. Spattering should be fairly heavy.

Dry-brushing

This texturing technique is particularly useful on woodwork or to produce a woodwork effect. First, the painter must have a dry brush. The brush is dipped very lightly in the paint and dragged across the surface to be treated. Dry-brushing is usually done with a single color: dark brown, black, or dark gray. It takes some practice to develop a good dry-brush technique, but the effect is well worth the time. (See Fig. 25 for effects of spattering and dry-brushing.)

Spraying and Sprayers

Spraying is a quick method of achieving results similar to spattering. The use of hand fly-spray guns is not usually effective. Occasionally, one of the more expensive large-capacity models will work for a while, but eventually the nozzle will clog. Paint used in spray guns should be thinned down considerably and stirred thoroughly so that there are no lumps. Spraying should be done ten to eighteen inches from the flat, depending on the kind of gun. The large tank-type garden spray is one of the most dependable kinds of hand-operated sprayers. They are much more expensive to purchase but outlast many of the inexpensive fly-spray guns. The best spray gun is the electric type, and some models now are fairly inexpensive. This gun takes practice to use properly but it produces wonderful results. Needless to say, all spray guns should be cleaned completely after each spray coat. Spraying gives a much finer texture than spattering, and more colors can be used. Both spraying and spattering a set can produce some very effective texture results.

Caution

A word of caution about paints:

1. Do not use any form of *enamel* or *oil-base* paint on flats (unless you are ready to throw them away after one show). Oil-base paints do not "paint over" on muslin.

2. Do not use spray cans of paint in gold or silver on flats. It is nearly impossible to paint over gold or silver paints.

3. Avoid latex (rubber-base) paints except for door frames and furniture. It builds up on flats, makes them sag, and gives them a shiny appearance under stage lights.

4. If several people on the scenery crew are painting, it is best that they work together and blend their work, since no two people paint alike.

5. No one learns to paint out of a book, this one or any other. Practice is the only way to perfect painting techniques.

Putting Scenery Together

Once the scenery has been constructed and painted, its placement on stage is the final step. Handling flats is a tricky business for those who have never handled them.

Too many stage-crew members want to pick up the flat and carry it alone wherever it is needed. Flats should only be carried by *two people*, one at either end of the flat. If you carry a flat alone, you run the dangers of personal injury, cracking the stiles or rails of the flat, ripping or tearing the muslin on other scenery,

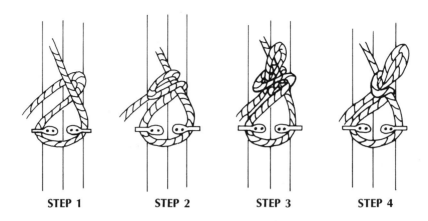

STEP 1   STEP 2   STEP 3   STEP 4

Fig. 26. Lashing tie-off.

and knocking down scenery already put up. When "running a flat," keep the bottom rail on the floor at all times, balance the flat with the "high hand," and push it where it is needed. Then wait for the scenery chairperson or stage manager to position the flat for assembly.

Lashing

Lashing flats together is the commonest and simplest method of putting scenery up. Each flat has a length of clothesline attached to the upper right-hand corner (as one looks at the back of the flat). Spaced at regular intervals below the lashline are "lash cleats" (see Fig. 26), over which the lashline is thrown or flipped by holding onto the lower end of the lashline and aiming for the top lash cleat with the natural loop created by the throw. Lashing requires a little practice, so crew members should not be discouraged if they miss the lash cleat a few times. Some stage managers or scenery chairpeople prefer to lash with the aid of a stepladder. The lashline is then moved from one cleat to the other. The bottom cleats on most flats are called "tie-off" cleats and are somewhat thinner than the regular lash cleat. After all cleats have been included in the lashline, a tie-off is made according to Fig. 26. You should remember to keep the lashline as tight as possible during the entire process, including the tie-off. A little practice lashing and tieing-off will make most members of the stage crew proficient after one play.

Nailing

Nailing scenery together is another method of assembly. Nailing, however, presents a safety problem. To nail flats together in pairs, it is necessary to place the flat face down on the stage and use short scraps of 1″ × 3″ as the joiner. It is best if the flats are joined in at least three places — top, bottom, and at the middle above the toggle bar. Occasionally, two flats will meet at 90°, more or less, and you can join these by placing a six-penny (6 d) nail in the stile at the top, bottom, and middle. Make certain that the nail hits the edge of the stile of the second flat in this process. It is best not to drive the nail all the way in, but to leave just enough of the head out so that it can be removed with a claw hammer. A supply of double-headed nails, 6 or 8 d, can be kept on hand for this purpose. The nailing method of assembly should not be used if the set is to be changed during the play or if it is necessary to clear the stage for other activities before the actual production date. Since this situation occurs in most schools, it is recommended that the flats be nailed in pairs so the set

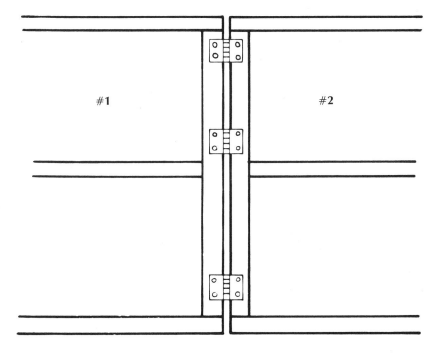

Fig. 27. Hinging flats.

can quickly be reassembled without repeating the entire nailing process.

Hinging

Hinging flats together is a third method of assembly. Drop-pin or loose-pin hinges are used in all hinging on the stage (see Fig. 27). The reason for this should be quite clear. All flats must come apart for easy storage, and unless the flats are built as two- or threefolds they cannot be folded completely. In putting hinges on the flats for assembly purposes, they must be attached at a standard distance from the top and the bottom of the flat. Flats are not always assembled in the same order for each production, and they should be interchangeable with one another. While hinging has many apparent advantages, cost is not one of them. It will cost more than a dollar to put hinges on each flat. Another disadvantage is that, no matter how hard the stage crew tries, not all flats are going to assemble with hinges alone. Matching up hinges on ten flats so that all interchange is nearly impossible; the set always assembles best the way it was done originally. Hinging works best on twofold and threefold flats, intended to be permanently hinged together. In making this assembly, it is necessary to use a "jigger," a 1″ × 2″ strip placed between the two flats to facilitate folding (see Fig. 28).

Large walls may be assembled by using a "stiffener" (a long length of 1″ × 3″) and a "keeper hook" (see Fig. 29). The keeper hook is a piece, usually of ½″ wide flat-iron, bent to an S shape to slide over the toggle bar of the flat. In assembling three flats, it is necessary to have three keepers, one for each flat, placed in the center of the toggle bar, and the 1″ × 3″ stiffener is dropped in the bottom loop of the S.

Large straight walls of three or more flats may be assembled by using a stiffener (a long length of 1″ × 3″) placed across the back of all the flats of the wall and nailed to each individual flat in several places with double-headed nails. Usually two stiffeners are needed to give the wall sufficient rigidity and stability. Care should be taken not to drive the nails through the flat, but in just far enough to secure a bond.

Of the three methods of assembly, lashing is by far the easiest and the cheapest. Clothesline is relatively inexpensive and 8 and 10 nails can be substituted for lash cleats if necessary. Stage

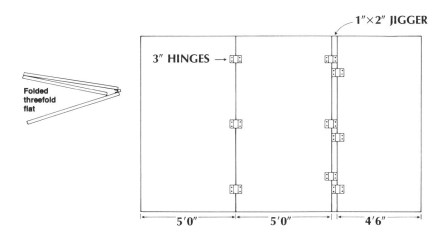

Fig. 28. Threefold flats.

Fig. 29. Hinged panorama set for *Oklahoma*, Western Michigan University, James W. Miller Auditorium. Directed by William Livingston, designed by Roy Beck.

managers and directors for years have sought to find easier methods, but they nearly always return to lashing as the best way.

Dutchmanning

Once the entire set is up or the set pieces are in place, the "dutchmanning" process is next. Dutchmanning is adding 4″ or 5″ strips of muslin (dipped in the base paint) to the seams where flats are joined together. The dutchman strip is usually soaked in the base paint so that the paint oozes through the cloth fibers. The strip is then applied to the seam by hand or with a brush. This is a messy process, and care should be taken to protect the stage floor and the rest of the set. Since dutchmanning is one of the last things to be done to the set, it is frequently omitted. Most audiences will accept a stage setting for what it is: an illusion of reality. Well-made flats usually are joined together with a fine seam, and dutchmanning should be used only where *extreme* realism is required. Permanent two- and threefolds flats should be dutchmanned when they are made; these will be painted as the set is painted and will require no other treatment.

Bracing

At certain key points, all sets need to be braced with stage braces or homemade versions of stage braces (see Fig. 30). Entrances require bracing on both sides of the door (hinged and opening). Long flat walls require at least one brace, and frequently the windows need bracing. A commercial stage brace, either of wood or aluminum, lasts for years. The hook at the top of the brace is inserted upside down into the brace cleat on the flat and turned 180° so that the brace rests against the flat stile and the brace cleat. These directions are important! A misapplied brace can ruin weeks of work by ripping through the muslin covering with the first jar the brace gets backstage. The "rocker" end of the stage brace is either screwed to the stage floor with a stage screw or nailed with #10 or #12 nails and toed over. The adjustment in the center of the brace provides for making certain the flat stands straight and does not tilt backward or forward. Be certain the thumb screw is tight once the flat stands straight.

In many schools, nailing into the stage floor or drilling holes for stage screws is strictly forbidden. In other schools, the stage

Fig. 30. Adjustable stage brace.

Fig. 31. Non-skid floor plate.

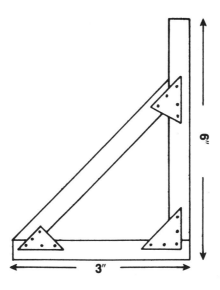

Fig. 32. Scenery jack.

floor is made of regular hardwood flooring instead of softwood, as recommended by theatre architects. How does a play-producing group cope with these problems? You can just go ahead and do it, or you can find another method of bracing the set. One manufacturer of stage hardware has perfected a "non-skid floor plate" for use with stage braces (see Fig. 31). These are useful on hardwood or tile floors. Another method is to build a bracing strip of 2″ × 4″s lashed to the back and side walls of the stage so the set is braced from the top rail of the flat to the bracing strip.

Other methods of bracing are making pseudo-stage braces of 1″ × 3″s in a T shape and nailing them to the flat stile edge. Set pieces may be braced with a stage brace or may be held upright by means of scenery jacks. A scenery jack is made of 1″ × 3″s in a triangle shape in varying heights, according to the height of the flat or set piece (see Fig. 32). The height of the jack is usually twice that of the base, but this may vary according to backstage conditions. Jacks are attached to the flat at the toggle bar with hinges. The flat should be laid face down on the stage, and the jack laid on the flat ½″ from the bottom rail. The ½″ provides space for the flat to rock back, and the weight of the flat is carried on the back one-third of the jack. Sometimes jacks are attached to both right and left stiles, and sandbags are used to weight them down. It is not usually necessary to nail or screw scenery jacks to the stage floor.

Shifting Sets

Some plays and most musicals require more than one set, and it is necessary to *shift* scenery during the progress of the play. The shifting of any scenery requires detailed planning by the director and the stage crew. Each crew member must know exactly what he or she is to do to complete the shift. A "shifting chart" can be used to record each crew member's specific task.

There are two basic ways of shifting scenery. First, you can "strike" (take down) set number one completely, usually starting at the two downstage sides and removing the set, flat by flat (or unit by unit if flats are nailed or hinged together). If the set has a back wall, it may be removed intact and stored on the back wall of the stage. In shifting, care should be taken not to cover up set number two. Silly as that may sound, it has happened to stage crews in a big hurry to make the shift. The second method of shifting is by placing set number two "inside" set number one (see Fig. 33). This method is quite effective, provided the second set is smaller and requires less acting area than set number one.

In making this shift, an entrance is made from the backstage area by removing certain flats of set number one near the storage area for set number two. All furniture and props from set number one are removed completely or are pushed far enough back to permit set number two to be set up. Work should begin from the point farthest from the backstage entrance to the point nearest the entrance. If large props are used in set number two, they should be put in *first* and pushed down to the curtain line out of the crew's way until the second set is completely up. The "set within a set" method of shifting is one of the better methods and is the one that should be tried, especially if later action of the play returns to set number one. *Shifting of scenery must be practical, not taken for granted!*

Sets requiring shifting should not be nailed together — hammering onstage is very disconcerting to an audience. Practice the set shifting at least twice, and more if time permits. Shifting should be done as quietly and quickly as possible. Remember, a shift that takes a crew five minutes to make seems like fifteen to an audience seated in a dark auditorium. For very long shifts, planned intermissions to "cover" the shift should be used. Sometimes a musical interlude can help the audince pass the time during scene changes. (See section on "Sound Effects".)

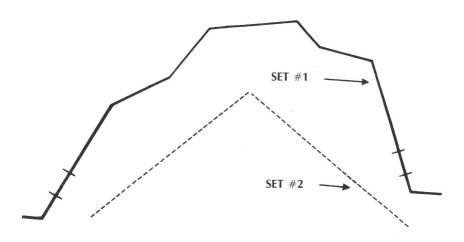

Fig. 33. A set within a set.

Shifting Arena Settings

In arena staging, scene shifts must take place in full view of the audience. No attempt should be made to "sneak" scene changes, but the changes should be made as quickly and quietly as possible. The people making the changes should know exactly what they are to do. They should not put on an "extra performance" for the audience. (Sometimes all stagehands dress alike, in coveralls or in costumes.) Stagehands should not wear the "grubbies" usually worn backstage on the traditional stage.

The placement of furniture and large set props can be marked on the floor with masking tape and labeled, or if there are a number of changes, the tape can be color-coded and the pieces marked with a piece of tape of the same color. If changes must be made in darkness or semi-darkness, phosphorescent tape or paint can be used to mark the placement of furniture and props on the stage floor. Two final words of advice: *plan* and *practice* scene changes.

Properties

Properties are of two basic types: the *large-set property*, which is really a part of the stage setting, and the *small hand prop*. It is the first type that is discussed here. Properties are defined as any part of the stage setting which is movable and not a part of the flats per se. The purpose of properties is to aid the audience in the location and time of the play. You will remember that we said that location and time are the two important functions of scenery. Properties, likewise, serve the same purpose. Set props are usually selected by the properties crew according to a list that appears in the back of most play books. These in part are hand props, and in some cases set props. Set props are considered to be the furnishing of the scenery, making the set complete, and as such they should fix the period in which the action of the play takes place. Do not make the serious error of having properties that do not fit the play. Time and again, plays supposedly taking place during the 1900s are furnished with props of the 1970s and 1980s. This is most incongruous and does not aid the audience's understanding of either the location or the time.

Most prop crews are not familiar with all furniture styles,

especially period furniture. By consulting one of the leading furniture stores on period styles, you will ensure getting the correct style to fit the play. Properties may either be borrowed or made for a particular production. It is recommended that you borrow whenever possible and make properties only as a last resort. It sometimes is necessary to call upon friends of the prop crew in order to supply the furnishings, and many people have stored in their attic, basement, or garage a surplus of furniture. It is on this surplus that a prop crew often must draw. As you begin your work, understand clearly that the furnishings, as hand props, must fit the period of the play. Do not blindly accept the first pieces of furnishings offered to you if you can tactfully refuse. A prop crew should use all the devices at its disposal to locate props. First, contact members of the cast and see if they have the necessary pieces of furniture. Perhaps the director of the play has already located some of the more important pieces. In this case, it is up to you to call upon the owners and make arrangements for the props to be moved.

Props and some smaller furnishing do not have to be the real thing. For example, a play may call for a butter churn, but a butter churn can easily be made with a broomstick and a basket. Many times a prop is not seen in its entirety by the audience and, therefore, may be a facsimile. When set props are vital to the plot of the play, it is important to use pieces as authentic as possible.

A few more directions for the property crew. Make a complete list of the properties used, who supplied the props, and carefully note the condition of the props when they are picked up. Labels should be placed on most props to indicate ownership. Sometimes properties become damaged. It is then your responsibility to tell the director and to indicate that the property has a certain value placed on it by the owner. In some communities, furniture stores (furniture is by far the hardest of set props to acquire) will loan furniture to the dramatic group. Sometimes this borrowing can be accomplished by telling the store manager or owner that he or she will receive due credit on the program along with the cast's and crew's thanks for the contribution to the play. The merchant receives free publicity in the eyes of many playgoers, and stores who lend furniture to a school group usually are looked upon with favor by members of the community.

Using Plastic, Foam, and Metal Onstage

Modern chemistry has provided us with a large number of plastic and foam products for use in the home, industry, and building trades. Some of these products can be used on the stage for making props, set pieces and set decoration. *However, not all plastic or foam products should be used on the stage!*

Plastics

All plastics fall into two groups, soft or hard. The soft plastics are pliable, movable, and bend rather easily (some always returning to their molded shape). The hard plastics are rigid, difficult to bend, and nearly always keep their original shape unless they are heated or cut. Examples of soft plastics are Vis-Queen, a polyethylene plastic sheeting in either clear or black color, used by the construction industry as covering material for concrete and to hold insulation in place. Vis-Queen comes in rolls from 3' to 12' wide. On the stage, Vis-Queen has been used for entire sets. As free-form columns, it has been draped from battens to the stage floor creating eerie and unusual effects. The plastic has been cut in narrow strip and hung from the upper stage area to serve as a forest where the leaves are moving constantly. Care must be taken with lighting, since the shiny surface of Vis-Queen will reflect light into the audience. Most soft plastics of this kind tear easily, so a thin cardboard strip should be used between the plastic and the wood form when it is stapled or nailed. Since many plastics melt, they should be kept away from hot lights and flame.

Hard plastics (usually acrylics) appear to have a greater number of stage applications, and more are tried each season. Plexiglass and acrylic glass are used in many commercial and home applications, from basketball backboards to unbreakable storm doors and furniture. Most acrylics can be cut with a fine blade saw. Usually the thinner thicknesses should be scored first with a trim knife to ensure a clean cut. Odd shapes and free-forms should be cut *slowly*, since the material will crack. If cube shapes, frequently used as set pieces, are to be used by actors to stand or sit on, it is best to use thicker stock of ¼" or more and frame the object in either aluminum or wood. The home use of rigid plastics for room dividers and covered patios also provides some interesting applications for the stage. Colored panels can be used to create stained glass windows in such plays as *Becket* and *St. Joan.*

One of the more interesting new products is plastic plumbing pipe, PVC and CPVC. Already there is commercially made lawn furniture from the white plastic pipe. The pipe is easy to cut with a hacksaw or sabre saw, and a special cement is required to make the joint secure. The CPVC system includes pipe from ½″ to ¾″ in diameter with a wide assortment of "elbows" and "unions" for joining the pipe. It comes in 10′ lengths. The PVC system includes pipe from 1½″ to 8″ in diameter; it also comes in 10′ lengths. The process for bending the pipe is very difficult and should not be attempted by students. While it takes a little longer, cutting and gluing is the safer and surer method. The pipe can be used for barred window effects, handrails, modernistic or stylized trees, and columns. The uses of CPVC and PVC pipe are limited only by your imagination.

Foams

There are two basic types of foam plastics on the market, low-density and high-density. Density is the number and size of air cells injected into the plastic foam as it is formed; larger air cells are low-density, smaller air cells are high-density. Styrofoam is a low-density rigid foam. Urethane is a high-density rigid foam. Both types have many applications on the stage. Styrofoam has been used for a number of years in department store decorations and displays. Styrofoam is a lightweight, easily handled but quite brittle material and has very little strength. The foam comes in a wide variety of sizes and thicknesses. It can be glued together with white shop glue or polyvinyl glue to make extra-thick blocks. Cutting the styrofoam is best done with a trim knife or coping saw. Power saws tend to melt the foam, and it is a messy process. There are special "hot wire" cutters used by commercial display companies. The foam can be shaped with rasps, sandpaper, or a bernztorch. Sandpaper and rasps remove the foam, but the torch melts the foam. Therefore, torching should be done outdoors to provide adequate ventilation (the fumes should not be inhaled) and to keep the smell out of the building. Quite a few props, wall plaques, ornate moldings and cornices, and many three-dimensional objects can be made from styrofoam. Styrofoam is readily available from hardware, lumber, and discount stores, and from insulation firms.

Urethane is a high-density foam. It usually is sold in larger and thicker blocks than styrofoam. Urethane foam is easier to carve and shape than styrofoam with knives, power sanding discs and rasps, or woodcarving tools. Urethane is somewhat stronger than styrofoam and is less apt to break or crack during the forming stages. The uses are much the same as for styrofoam. However, the urethane product is much finer in detail and is more durable. Blocks of urethane can be glued together with a special cement (Dowmastic #11) to make statues, vases, etc. Urethane and styrofoam can be painted, but they require a prime coat of casein paint before the stage paint or artist colors are added.

Instant Foams

Aerosol cans of instant foam are available today at most hardware and discount stores. The foam is made to fill in cracks around window and door jambs in the home. The foam can be used onstage to create raised surfaces on scenery, such as the plaster falling out in a ramshackle house. Tree stumps and rock forms of wood and chicken wire with one layer of papier mâché can be sprayed with the foam to create the rough texture of the tree bark or rocks. The foam is a semi-liquid when it comes from the can and must be worked rather quickly as it hardens rapidly. The foam will stick to almost any surface except polyethylene plastics, wax, or teflon. Molds, such as those used in pottery, can be used to make hand props, or the foam can be sprayed over the real object to make a model. Molds should be lined with polyethylene, and objects should be wrapped in the plastic before applying the spray. Once the foam has set, the foam surface can be cut in two places to free it from the object. Then the two pieces can be put together and the cuts sprayed lightly. There are several theatre supply companies marketing a foam pack containing a large amount of the foam. The foams available in hardware stores will give one a good idea of how useful it will be for your play producing group. It is expensive, and costs much more than a sheet of styrofoam, but its use is different.

Celastic and Fiberglass

These two materials are actually fabrics with plastic treated surfaces that require a solvent to make them pliable enough to conform to a shape. Celastic is a special cheesecloth treated with cellulose nitrate, which when dipped in the special solvent becomes very pliable. One of the major uses of celastic on the stage has been making masks for Greek dramas. In addition, it has been used to cover rocks and trees. Since it is a fabric, it can be used directly on the wooden forms without a chicken wire or papier mâché base. When making models or duplicates of a prop, be sure to cover the real object with aluminum foil before applying the celastic. When the model is dry, cut the celastic in two places as was done in instant foam modeling, and apply strips of celastic over the cuts to make the model a single unit. Celastic is available by the yard from theatre supply houses.

Fiberglass sheets similar to those used for boat and auto body repair can be formed and shaped much like celastic. Fiberglass does come in several weights: light, medium, and heavy. The lighter weights can be used in much the same way celastic is used; the heavy weight material is especially good for making armor and shields as the knights of old used. Some fiberglass requires a two-step application to form it: a resin is applied to make the fiberglass sheets pliable so it can be formed, then a hardener is applied once the object is formed. While it sets quickly, fiberglass does require drying time. In a few newer types of fiberglass, the resin and hardener are mixed at one time. Fiberglass boat repair kits and auto body kits are usually available to experiment with before purchasing larger amounts.

Vacuum Formed Plastics
Should the theatre group decide not to make their own props, armor, or headdresses from the materials just described, they can buy vacuum formed plastic items. Several theatre supply houses specialize in vacuum formed materials. Vacuum forming is a complex process and requires expensive equipment to produce. A special plastic material is placed over a mold; then a vacuum is created between the plastic and the mold. With the addition of heat, the plastic is molded.

Metals
In some form or shape, metal has been used on the stage for

centuries. Primarily, its use has been in the off stage, or backstage areas as a built-in part of the stage proper. Pipe is one of the most useful shaped metals. Pipe is used as support for heavy platforms; as mounting for nearly all spotlights and floodlights; to weight scenery drops; as stands for spotlights; and some designers have made entire sets of pipe structures. Pipe comes in several lengths (10' and 20' are the most common). Pipe requires cutting and threading with special equipment. It is joined together with a larger variety of "elbows, nipples, and unions." Because of the strength of pipe, it has been used as a support material, and it has been used as legs for commercially made platforms.

Angle metals have been used for many years as a part of the architectural structure of most theatres and auditoriums. The prime difficulty in using them for onstage purposes has been the need to weld them. In the late 1950s a slotted steel angle was introduced from Great Britain, using a series of engineered slots and holes and bolted together. The trade name, Dexion, became the "erector set of industry" for countless industrial applications that once required angle iron and welding. There are several good slotted angle "packages" on the market today for the making of dollies, carts, racks, platforms, as bracing for scenery, mounting spotlights in areas where pipe could not be used, and many other uses. One of the major advantages of the slotted angle is it can be taken apart and reused in new ways on the stage.

Thin-wall Conduit
In recent years some designers have used this electrical installation material as free-form objects, as stylized trees, and as parts of stage sets. Thin-wall conduit (TWC) cuts easily with a hacksaw, and it can be bent with a conduit bender. It comes in sizes from ½" to 3", the cost is not too great, and there is always a possibility of recovering part of the cost by selling the conduit to local electrical contractors.

In addition to the pipe, angle, and thin-wall described here, there are U shapes and channel metals that can be readily adapted for use on the stage; in fact many lighting companies use electrically wired channels as a part of their systems.

As with all equipment on the stage, safety should be a major factor; safety for the stage crew making the set or object, and safety for the actors who must use it. The volatile and unstable nature of most plastic materials requires the utmost safety in handling. Sharp metal edges on most metals can cut very easily, so the edges should be taped to prevent actors from cutting themselves. Safety glasses should be worn whenever stage crew members cut any material: wood, plastic, or metal.

Stage Lighting

Stage lighting has several important purposes. First of all, an audience comes to *see* a play. Second, in each play there is a certain *mood* which must be conveyed by means of the setting and the lighting. Third, lighting should convey *time:* daylight, dawn, night, bright sunlight, etc. Fourth, *special effects* are created by lighting: shadows, lightning, explosions, etc. There are, then, four purposes for lighting the stage: visibility, mood, time, and special effects. An audience should not have to strain to see the actors on the stage, nor should the stage be so brightly lit as to cause the audience to hide its eyes momentarily to avoid eyestrain. While these may seem to be extreme examples, they can happen in your play. The happy medium is difficult to achieve in the brief time that you will have to spend in play production.

In order for the four purposes to be conveyed on the stage, two things are necessary: good *equipment* and adequate *control*. Equipment for stage lighting consists of the following lighting instruments: spotlight, floodlights, border lights, follow spots, and footlights. Control consists of the switchboard and dimming equipment.

Lighting instruments

The spotlight is the basic lighting instrument that is used to light the acting areas of the stage, three upstage and three downstage. "Spots," as they are called, come in four basic types: plano-convex, Fresnel, ellipsoidal, and sealed beam (see Fig. 34).

The plano-convex spotlight was one of the first spotlight developments after incandescent lights were introduced on the stage. Its primary features are an aluminum reflector, a globe-shape lamp, and a plano-convex lens. The wattage of the lamp varies from 250 to 2,000 watts. The effective "throw" of the light is from 10 feet to 100 feet. A "hard edge" circle of light is formed by the

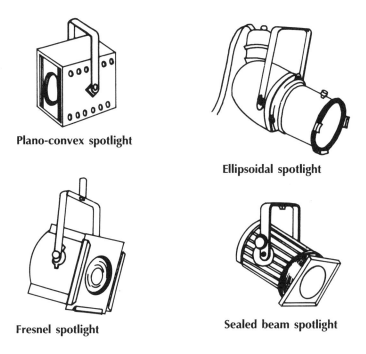

Plano-convex spotlight

Ellipsoidal spotlight

Fresnel spotlight

Sealed beam spotlight

Fig. 34. Four types of spotlights.

plano lens. Planos are most effective when hung from the first batten behind the act curtain.

The Fresnel spotlight also derives its name from its lens. Its primary features are an aluminum reflector (larger than the plano's), a T-shape lamp, and a lens that has a series of vertical planes and either dots or stripes stippled on the lens. The wattage of the Fresnel is usually 500 watts for onstage purposes and up to 1,500 watts for out-front lighting. The effective throw for a 6″ Fresnel on the first batten is up to 25 feet. For the larger Fresnels, with 8″ and 10″ lenses, the throw is up to 60 feet. The Fresnel lens gives the light beam a soft or feathered edge — a clear circle of light is not distinguishable. Six-inch and 8″ lenses are most effective onstage, and 10″ lenses and over serve best from out front.

The ellipsoidal spotlight employs two devices: first is the elliptical reflector and the second is the T-type lamp that burns "base up." By combining the elliptic reflector and the T-lamp, the spotlight produces a highly efficient and concentrated beam of light. The beam is directed by a shutter or iris system between the lamp and the lens. Wattage of ellipsoidals, or "lekos" as they are sometimes called, varies from 250 to 2,000 watts, depending upon lens sizes and the throw desired. Lekos serve best from out front and are usually used to light the front acting areas.

The fourth type of spotlight is a recent development: the sealed-beam spotlight. Its origin is largely industrial and "automotive." The headlights of family cars, for example, have sealed beams. Most schools have some kind of outdoor night lighting that employs sealed beams. As the name implies, the lamp and the lens are sealed in one unit. This used to be a disadvantage for use on the stage. By developing new types of lenses and filaments, lighting manufacturers were able to refine the sealed beam to satisfy most school stage lighting needs. Some sealed-beam units employ an additional lens system to increase the output of the unit. Sealed-beam lights may be used onstage or out front. Their effective throw depends on their wattage, which is deceptively low: 75 to 500 watts. The same-watt sealed-beam lamp may be used onstage or out front, and the only adaptation needed is in the length of the light housing: the longer the housing, the longer the throw. The use of another lens system superimposed on the sealed-beam lamp can produce very effective results up to 50 feet.

Sealed-beam lights offer several advantages not provided by traditional stage spotlights. First, they are inexpensive initially, in

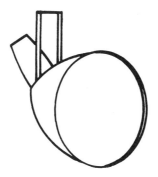

Fig. 35. Scoop floodlight.

upkeep, and to burn. Second, they are lightweight and easily handled. Third, lamp replacements are readily available from most local commercial electrical contractors. Schools not having adequate lighting facilities or those planning to remodel older installations should by all means consider sealed-beam lights.

Floodlights provide light for the stage in a wide angle. Floods are usually used for backlighting and cyclorama lighting. Flood-lights do not have a lens system but have reflectors that cover the entire inside surface of the instrument. Floodlights have a short throw, not more than 15 feet effective distance. Floods may be hung from battens or put on light stands. Sky cycloramas and ground rows are usually lit with floods. Occasionally school stages are not equipped with border lights and floodlights are used instead. Various names have been given to floods; "scoops" and "wizards" are two of the more common names (see Fig. 35).

The long trough of red, white, and blue lights are called border lights. Borders are hung on the stage in two places: on the first batten with the spotlights or immediately behind them, and about the middle of the stage behind the second border curtain. Border lights are made in two basic types: the *continuous reflector* type and the *individual reflector* type. The continuous reflector has a single reflecting surface running the length of the trough or strip. In the trough are placed colored lamps of from 60 to 150 watts. Individual-reflector-type border lights usually come in sections 6 to 12 feet long and may be hung on the first batten, separated by several spotlights. Each color is individually controlled at the switchboard. A new version of the border light has been recently introduced on the stage in the form of the small-wattage sealed beams, R-40s or PARs, in a housing that looks like a small spotlight. Wattage varies from 75 to 200 watts.

The purpose of border lights is to give *general illumination*, to *tone* and *blend* the acting areas. While most schools will probably have red, white, and blue lights in the border, the true light primary colors are red, green, and blue. Red, white, and blue, when mixed, never produce any light color except those shades of red and blue. However, red, green, and blue, when mixed, produce a wide range of color, from gray to white.

The follow spotlight (see Fig. 36) can be used in a number of ways to light the stage. Since the lighting instrument has "follow" in its name, the primary use has been to follow a single or several

Fig. 36. Follow spotlight.

performers as they move about the stage singing or dancing in musicals or variety shows. However, the follow spot can be used quite effectively in straight plays in several ways. The follow can be used to create special effects from a fixed position in a balcony, from a beam slot, or located in a lighting or projection booth. With the colored media (gels) and cut-out designs, "eerie" effects can be created on the stage for fantasy and suspense plays. The follow spot can also be used to spotlight a single important prop or piece of action that will help the audience understand the plot of the play better.

Several important features separate the follow spotlight from all other lighting instruments. The follow has a long hood or body, usually 30″ to 48″ for incandescent lamp models, and up to 6′ long for arc spotlights. In most cases, it is mounted on a rolling stand with large casters for smooth, easy movement. In addition, it is mounted so it can turn a full circle (360 degrees) very easily. It can move up and down with ease in the very large mounting yoke. Follow spotlights are usually the most powerful lights in the theatre lighting system; seldom are they less than 1000 watts and many are 2,000 watts or more. The powerful wattage of the incandescent lamp and the long hood combine to produce the longest throw of a light, from 100 feet up to 300 feet, depending on the lamp wattage. All follows are equipped with a movable iris, which controls the size of the pool of light projected on the stage. Many follows can "iris-down" to a head-spot of 15″ or 18″, and "iris-out" to a spread of 20′ to 30′, covering the full stage. On the top or side of the follow near the operator are a series of levers or buttons that control the color media (gels) built into the light by the manufacturer. Mixing the gels can create some "unusual" colored light on the stage. Some follow spots are equipped with four-way framing shutters to square off the usual circle of light for special effects. Unlike most spotlights that have a single lens, the follow spot has a series of two and many newer models have three lenses. One of the lenses can be moved by the operator to create a soft or hard edge on the light pool and adjust the size of the light pool as well.

Arc spotlights are usually found in large professional theatres and require special instruction to operate them safely and effectively.

Footlights, while an integral part of older stages, have been almost eliminated from modern lighting installations. If the stage is equipped with foots, their use is not usually recommended for several reasons. First, foots have a tendency to creat "skull" effects on the faces of the actors, making the eyes appear hollow and black. If tradition dictates that footlights should be used, it is recommended that they be dimmed very low. Today, with modern spotlights and adequate dimming equipment, footlights are a memory of the past.

Dimming Mechanisms

The dimming mechanism is next in importance to the lighting instruments. The purpose of the dimmer is to control the *level* of the lighting instruments — the brightness or dimness of the lamps in the spots, borders, or floods. The dimmers are usually housed in a complex called the switchboard, in which are located the main toggle switches or circuit-breakers for turning the lights on and off. A number of different types of dimmers are on the market today.

The *resistance* dimmer is the oldest type of dimming equipment to be found in most schools and auditoriums. The resistance system uses a number of different sized metal contact points of various thicknesses to control the amount of electrical current flowing to lighting instruments. The thicker the contact, the more resistance, the less electrical current flowing to the lights; the thinner the contact, the more current flows to the lights. Resistance dimmers are readily identifiable by their large size and circular shape. Usually the individual dimmers are "ganged" together with a larger master dimmer for all of the individual ones. There are a number of disadvantages to resistance dimmers compared with the newer types available today. Most resistance dimmers have a fixed load rating. (A load is the number of lighting instruments with proper lamp wattage to match the dimmer's rating.) To operate, the dimmer must have a minimum wattage load and cannot exceed the maximum wattage load without damage to the dimmer and blowing fuses. A large number of resistance dimmer installations have all light loads permanently wired to the dimmers to avoid the problem of under and over loads. This practice, while assuring safety, does not permit the kind of flexibility required by most stage lighting today. Another disadvantage of resistance dimmers is the need for service and maintenance, especially to the contact points on the radial surface as well as to the dimmer arm. The contact must be kept clean and firm; dust and a lack of firm contact can cause arcing. If the resistance dimming system is troublesome, one of the newer types described should be considered.

The *autotransformer* dimmer (see Fig. 37) was one of the next developments in lighting control. As the name implies, the dimming coil is a large transformer, much like the smaller ones used to control model railroads and slot cars. The advantage of the autotransformer is that it can dim any size load, up to the maximum wattage rating of the dimmer. For example, it can dim a 25 watt lamp or a total of 6,000 to 12,000 watts for a group of lamps, whichever is the maximum rating of the dimmer. The autotransformer has a number of advantages over the resistance type dimmer. It is lightweight and compact; indeed, many are sold as portable package dimmers. The autotransformer has very few moving parts internally, and thus requires very little maintenance. Most important, it is easy for students to operate. The portable

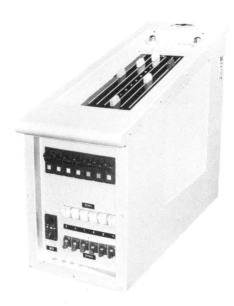

Fig. 37. Autotransformer dimmer. (Photo courtesy Electro-Controls, Ariel Davis Mfg. Division.)

package units are very useful for many school events and performances, such as dance programs, swimming programs, and fashion shows, in addition to their use for school theatre presentations in areas other than the auditorium or theatre.

The perfection of the transistor and miniaturization in the electronics industry have ushered in a new era of stage lighting control. In all electronic lighting control there are certain basic components. The arrangement of the components will vary from manufacturer to manufacturer, and there are a variety of add-on features. The add-on features can be compared to the optional equipment available in automobiles, such as automatic transmission, power brakes, power steering, etc. The optional equipment makes the car easier to drive; the add-on features make lighting control easier.

In most electronic systems, a step-down transformer is used to convert the 120-volt electrical current to low voltage (see Fig. 38). The low-voltage is used to operate the master control unit, all individual control units, and the add-on equipment. The low-

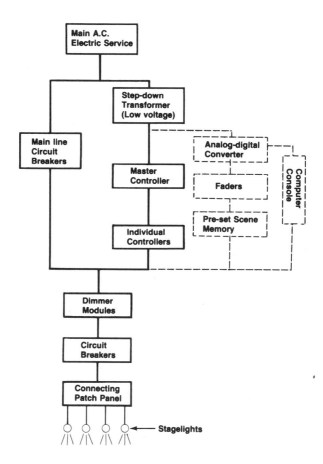

Fig. 38. Basic electronic control system (add-on features are indicated by broken lines).

voltage is joined to the 120-volt current at the dimmer modules. The connector panel, or plug-in strip, is used to connect individual spotlights to the various dimmers. The connector panel is arranged so that any light can be assigned to any dimmer and individual controller. The add-on features, such as faders, memory bank, pre-set scenes, and computer, are put into the basic system on the low-voltage side of the schematic. The introduction of micro-wave control by some companies can be compared to remote control units on television sets, or automatic garage door openers. A radio signal is sent from the control unit to the numbered dimmer, and the light dims up or down according to which direction the operator moves the slider. The garage door opener remote unit in the car opens the door when the button is pushed; it closes it in the same way. Since there are only two functions necessary in the garage door opener, it is easy to understand. In the electronic dimmer, the garage door opener principle is multiplied many times. These are some of the more recent developments in electronic control of lighting. In the process of arriving at electronic control there were earlier developments.

After the introduction of the autotransformer dimmer, the *silicon controlled rectifier* was the next step (see Fig. 39). The SCR dimmer is one of the more popular dimmers on the market today for replacing old dimming systems as well as new installations. SCR uses a solid state circuitry and a type of transistor that has a large capacity and is heavy-duty at the heart of the system. While the transistor is heavy-duty and lightweight, it is not very expensive to produce. In addition, it requires almost no maintenance and has a very long life. The disadvantages of the SCR system are that it is rather delicate to handle, especially when determining dimmer loads and setting up the dimmer; and the SCR generates heat, so that some type of fan venting system must be used in the lighting booth or backstage to remove the heat. Some recent changes have helped these two disadvantages. Because of its size, efficiency, and cost, it is easy to understand why the SCR is so popular.

The final phase of electronic lighting control is still in process. Major lighting firms have introduced computer controlled dimming packages. Presently, there are only a few schools in the nation with this type of dimming control. The addition of the computer into the system permits a visual graphic display of light level or a computer print-out sheet as quickly as the program for a given scene is activated.

Some systems are using a program either on disc or on magnetic or metal tape; others are using a punch card system. The disc/tape system is set up during the rehearsals by the lighting director or director, and the final show program is made from the rehearsal practice sessions. In all of the electronic boards, "channels" are used to refer to the number of dimmer capacities. In electric

Fig. 39. Silicon rectifier dimmer.

dimmer boards, these are referred to as "circuits." Quite a few of the electronic boards feature a pre-set scene module, permitting the operator to set up the lighting for scenes well in advance and at the proper moment push the activate button on the console and light the stage as pre-planned. The number of pre-set scenes varies with the type of console.

Nearly all of the electronic boards feature a "manual override system," so that the operator can take over the computer, memory bank, or pre-set scene module and manually change or rearrange the lighting for the scene. There is a repeat scene feature with some of the boards, so the operator can go back and repeat a scene during rehearsals by touching the repeat button. A small hand-held remote satellite dimmer — no larger than a hand calculator — which can be used while seated in the theatre, is featured by some boards.

Regardless of the type of dimming control used, it is necessary to connect the lighting instrument to the dimming equipment. Most switchboards do this via a patch-panel or quick-connect panel (see Fig. 40). The principle employed by both is the same. In the patch-panel, a cord is plugged into the dimming circuit the

Fig. 40. Quick-connect panel.

operator wants to use; then it is plugged into the light circuit wanted. All light circuits terminate in a panel, so it is possible to connect any light circuit to any dimmer. The quick-connect panel differs in that no cords are involved in connecting the light circuit to the dimmer circuit. Instead, a series of buss bars, in a criss-cross fashion, permit the operator to use a contact slider to connect any two circuits with proper positioning (usually a numbered or lettered stop).

Permanently wired light circuits usually are the rule in most schools, and lighting crews are faced with the problem of getting instruments off the circuit or adding more to it. Sometimes it is necessary to cut cables of permanently wired circuits to get more flexibility, but this should be done only by a qualified electrician or school maintenance staff member. If cable splicing is not possible to gain flexibility, there is the option of using a mutliple branch-off connector. This useful connector permits the lighting crew to plug in three light instruments into a single fixed circuit. *Care must be taken not to overload the circuit* with more wattage than it was designed to carry.

Lamps

All lighting instruments have a source of light; this is called a *lamp*. Commonly, it is referred to as a light bulb. Actually, the

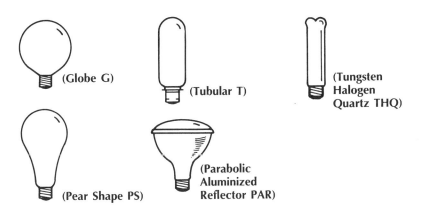

Fig. 41. Lamp shapes.

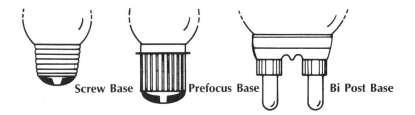

Fig. 42. Types of lamp bases.

bulb is only the glass cylinder in which the filament is encased. Stage lamps have several parts: the bulb that varies in shape (see Fig. 41), the filament which converts the electrical impulse into light, and the base which varies as to type (see Fig. 42). Each shape and base have specific uses in stage lighting. Some spotlights take a specific lamp and no other type can be used.

Plano-convex spotlights usually take a G-shape only in order for the reflector in the spotlight to correctly direct the light rays. The base of G-shape lamps will vary according to the lamp's wattage and the manufacturer; they are either screw base or prefocus base. Fresnel spotlights take a modified T-shape lamp with a prefocus base. Ellipsoidal spotlights use a T-shape lamp with a prefocus base that must be burned in the base-up position only. The ellipsoidal reflector will not collect the light rays if any other lamp is used. If the lamp is burned in any position but up, it will burn out very quickly (usually a matter of three hours and sometimes immediately). The wattage of stage lamps (and most home light bulbs) is determined by the diameter of the bulb of the lamp. Therefore, the larger the bulb of the lamp, the larger the wattage.

The industrial development of the tungsten-halogen lamp in the late 1950s has revolutionized stage lighting. The use of a tungsten filament, as is used in traditional incandescent lamps, with a halogen gas encased in a quartz glass bulb provides nearly 10 percent more light intensity than any other stage lamp. In addition, the size of the lamp bulb is greatly reduced to permit the halogen and quartz to electrically and chemically interact. This interaction replaces the tungsten on the filament. Thus, by adding halogen and quartz, the life of the lamp is increased three times over an incandescent lamp of the same wattage. For years, stage lamps have had a very short life (the amount of hours the lamp will burn before it burns out). The tungsten-halogen lamp has changed that. The positions just given for the Fresnel and ellipsoidal spotlights do not apply to the tungsten-halogen lamps; they may be burned in any position.

Today lamp manufacturers are producing tungsten lamps in many of the shapes illustrated here, and in several newer shapes for special applications. A new borderlight using a tungsten-halogen lamp, which looks like an automotive fuse with contacts on each end, clips into the borderlight reflector. The change in stage lighting is not over; there are experiments with controlled laser beams for stage use underway in several laboratories. Since all stage lighting lamps contain gases, they must be handled with a great deal of care. Whenever you or members of the lighting crew clean or change lamps or lenses in spotlights or borderlights, always wear a pair of heavy leather work gloves in the event a lamp should break or explode.

Lighting Plot
Figure 43 represents a basic method of lighting the six acting areas. The upstage areas are lit from the first batten and the downstage areas are lit from out front. This is *basic* lighting, and special requirements for each play will require additional lights.

A *lighting plot* shows the location of lights, the color of each instrument, the area at which it is directed, wattage amounts, and the special effect for which it is to be used. Plots should be worked out with the costume and make-up crews so that the color media do not clash with or "wash out" costume or make-up color. Most lighting plots are tentative to begin with and are finalized during dress rehearsals and technical rehearsals. Before every play, the light crew should determine the lighting needs of the play and make out a lighting plot.

Setting Lights
At least three people are necessary to set lights properly. Either the director or light-crew chairperson should "walk" the acting areas to make certain the lights are set at the right level. With a crew member on the control board and one on a ladder, the upstage lights should be set for up-and-down movement by

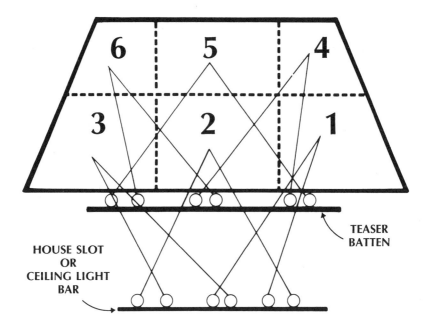

Fig. 43. Cross spotlighting.

loosening the large thumbscrews or hex bolts on either side of the spot. For right-left moves there may be either a ⁹⁄₁₆″ hex-head bolt or a ³⁄₄″ nut on a pipe. The person sitting on the ladder should have a pair of leather-palmed gloves and either vise-grip pliers or an adjustable wrench. The person "walking" the areas should fix his or her gaze at the light and look for the filament in the light. Once the filament is located (this takes practice and experience), it should be centered so that the viewer sees circles or rings as he or she gazes at it. At this point, the highest intensity to be used on this light during the show should be tested. Once the light is set, the color frame should be inserted so that the walker can get an idea as to proper color media. After each area is set, the third person on the control board either dims out or turns off that area and brings up the next area. Front lights are set in the same way, with the sitting either in the "slot" or on a scaffold. Setting the lights takes time; it should *not* be left until dress rehearsal. Once all areas are set, the walker should check for dark spots or unwanted shadows. If the area is lit properly, there should be two shadows in the light pool from 60° to 90° apart.

Having developed a lighting plot and set the lights, the crew should make a light-cue sheet, nothing the lighting changes required and specific instructions by the director for each scene or act of the play. Members of the light crew must know their specific jobs during the play. Figure 44 is a sample light-cue entry.

Act I, Scene 1

Cue: Change:

George: But Tom, it is impossible.   BLACK OUT: Take down 1, 2, 3, 4, 5, 6 dimmers completely.

Tom: Hey! What happened?

George: Storm must be heading our   SOUND CUE: Thunder.
way.   LIGHTNING: Flash switch 21 on and off rapidly.

Cues may be lines, as above, or
movements such as: George walks   Bring all dimmers up to 8½.
DR; flips switch.

Fig. 44. Lighting cue sheet.

Running Lights
Hints for operators:

1. Lights should move up and down smoothly, not too rapidly. The human eye opens and closes at various speeds, depending on many factors. Consider the comfort of the audience seated in a darkened auditorium.

2. House and stage lights should dim up and down at about the same time for intermissions or at the end or beginning of an act. *Timing is very important.* An audience should not have to wait for the light person to find the house lights' switch or dimmer.

3. Opening the curtain and bringing up the stage lights should occur at the same time. As the curtain opens (assuming it opens on a fully lighted stage), the lights should come up so that when the curtain is fully open the lights are at the proper dimmer reading.

4. Beware of scenes too dimly or too brightly lit. If the set and furnishings are of warm colors, lights should as a rule be dimmed down a small amount.

5. *Practice light changes* so they come off smoothly and quietly, particularly if the switchboard is located backstage where noise can be heard by the audience.

6. Check out all lights before each performance. Sometimes key spots have shifted or moved because of curtain pulls or other events on the stage during the day. Occasionally lamps have burned out. The checkout should be early in the evening, before the audience arrives.

7. Run lights during rehearsals to give actors the feel of working under lights.

8. Check the switchboard after each performance to make sure it is completely off. Leaving a board on "dimmed down" all night can cause damage to dimmers, as well as being a fire hazard.

Running the lights is a big responsibility. Lighting crews should accept this responsibility and make certain that all equipment is kept in good operating condition at all times.

Arena Lighting

Unless your school is equipped with an arena stage and lighting facilities designed for it, you will have to make do with what lighting equipment is at hand. Some of the things about to be suggested can be kept and used again and again for arena productions. Others will work for a single show and can be returned to the lender. You will have to adapt the suggestions made here to your school's physical facilities, for it is not possible to discuss all situations in this volume. But a word of caution — audiences are fickle. Experiment with arena staging, by all means, but do not spend large sums of the dramatics budget on permanent equipment until you see whether or not the theatre-going community will attend arena productions.

To make what is at hand function as an arena lighting system, the following suggestions are made for using the gym floor as the arena.

1. Lighting poles can be made quickly from the volleyball standards used by the P.E. department. Poles can be placed at four points, usually one at each corner of the arena or at the entrances to the acting area. Lighting instruments can be placed on the stands 6″ to 8″ apart, or with just enough space to permit focusing. Once the instruments are on the poles, be sure to weight the base with sandbags or concrete blocks. The electric lines from the lights can be connected to a portable dimmer, or if the stage is located in the gymnasium they can be connected to the regular switchboard. Lights should be focused on the major acting areas, and care must be exercised to keep the light out of the audience's eyes. If it is not possible to light the area from one pole, try switching the area lights until you have the desired effect (without lighting the audience as well).

2. Mounting on basketball goals. Long throw spots (40′ or more) can be mounted on the backboards of basketball goals by using blocks of wood 1″ × 3″ and 2″ × 4″ where the C clamp makes contact. This will not hurt a metal or plexiglass backboard. Another method of mounting on the basketball goal is to raise the basket (quite a number of baskets are on a winch system) and mount the lights on the "locking bar" on the bottom of the basket. Again, you may need to use blocks to make the C clamp secure.

Methods 1 and 2 are makeshift; they involve a great deal of creative imagination on your part to work out the details. They require the cooperation of custodians and the P.E. department, and plenty of stage cable to make the long runs.

Another item that can be used is a pipe grid, hung from the gym ceiling by trapeze and ring ropes. The grid can be constructed of four 10′ lengths of 1½″ i.d. and four 90° elbows. This grid costs about $20 for pipe, but it will last for years. Be certain the grid is adequately balanced and all knots or wire clamps are secure. An operation of this nature must be under-taken *only* under the supervision of the head custodian and the P.E. coach.

Light poles similar to volleyball standards can be built. Make them taller than the volleyball stands, using 1½″ i.d. pipe. These can be made by plumbing shops or, if you are familiar with pipe cutting and threading, the stands can be made in the school shop. The bases of the stands are about 3' (four lengths of 1½' pipe), and four 90° elbows are used for feet. The stand requires a four-way tee. For stability with this size base, the height of the upright pipe should not exceed 12'.

It is, of course, possible to mount lights in many other ways for arena productions. Look around your school and locate places for mounting lights for arena productions.

Focusing lights in arena productions is a most important operation. Without borders to blend the areas, a number of shadows will be created using only spots. Unless these detract from the play's action, they should not be of major concern. The color media (gels) can be the same as for the traditional stage, warm colors from the actors' right and cool colors from the actors' left. This should depend on the major center of action. Extremely intense colors should be avoided in arena productions: magenta, deep amber, and the pure colors red to green.

Sound Systems

Squawk, squeal, and squeak sound systems have been characteristic of some theatres and auditoriums for quite a number of years. Many schools have older systems without sufficient power or flexibility for play production purposes. Except for the special speaker and principal's or dean's remarks to graduates, the sound system is used mainly by the play-producing group. Audiences today are much more aware of quality sound. The marketplace is overflowing with excellent sound systems for home use, and many members of the audience will have these in their homes. An excellent performance can be ruined by a poor, outdated sound system, and the audience disappointed and irritated.

The acoustical properties of each auditorium or theatre are different and require different kinds of systems. There are some general principles for upgrading the school sound system.

Power

A sound system should have ample power for all of the various applications for which it will be used. The basic amplifier should not be less than 250 watts, unless the auditorium is very small.

Extra power in a sound system is not wasted; it provides for the extras most sound systems should have.

Flexibility
The directions given in the sound effects section were designed for a school system *without* flexibility. The basic amplifier should have provision for tape recorders, turntables, and microphone mixers, in addition to at least four mike outlets. There should be ample speaker outlets as well, four at least, if not six.

Speakers
The larger the theatre or auditorium, the more speakers are necessary to get adequate sound coverage. It was once a saying in hi-fi circles, "a good speaker can make *any* system sound terrific!" Many hi-fi and stereo enthusiasts still believe in that saying when buying their home systems. They purchase excellent speakers and compromise on the other components. Speakers for an auditorium should be of high quality with multi-speaker ranges, and large enough to cover the area by angling the speakers for maximum coverage. The size of the woofer speaker should not be the only consideration. There are some who feel a 16″ woofer is better than a 12″ woofer. The type of driver mechanism and kind of enclosure are also important in selecting a speaker system.

Additions
As stated earlier, the system selected should provide for the addition of more equipment. In play production two items are really necessities: a turntable and a reel-to-reel tape recorder (not just a playback deck!). A microphone mixer enables the system to handle six to eight microphones from a single mike outlet on the amplifier. Many mixers are mini-power units, so they can handle the additional microphones. A school producing musicals each year will find a mixer an invaluable piece of sound equipment

Home or Professional Units
Should the school consider one of the home-designed sound systems readily available at sound discount houses? Perhaps! If the auditorium or theatre is small (seating 300 or less), then a large home system may work. The difference between the home

unit and the commercial unit is usually durability. For larger theatres or auditoriums, the professional commercial unit should be the first consideration. Professionally designed sound systems are customized for the specific theatre or auditorium by a sound engineer and a company offering consulting services.

Sound equipment, like the new electronic light boards, is sophisticated and complex and *should not be used by students not trained in the proper operation.* Training sessions should be given to students interested in learning how to operate the sound system or the light board. In this way, the drama group will always have trained technical personnel.

Sound Effects

A classic joke in the theatre illustrates the critical importance of timing sound effects. The villain pulls his gun from his pocket and says: "Charlie, I'm going to shoot you!" He squeezes the trigger, but nothing happens. "Charlie, I'm going to *shoot* you!" Again, nothing happens. "Charlie, I'm going to shoot you," the villain repeats louder, looking anxiously toward the wings. Still nothing happens. "All right, Charlie, I'm going to stab you," the villain shouts, pulling out his pocketknife and rushing toward Charlie. At this moment a loud shot is heard backstage. Sound effects are critical to any production and they must take place *on time.*

Sound-Cue Sheet
Your first duty as a sound-crew member is to make out a cue sheet, much like the lighting-cue sheet, and frequently your sound-cue sheet will be a part of the light-cue sheet. To make your sound-cue sheet, merely substitute the sound effect desired for the lighting change. Experience has shown that if one person makes out the cue sheet, it works better than having many persons do it. Sound crews, by the way, need not be big crews; two or three people with a knowledge of electronics and a good sense of timing can form an efficient team. Once the cue sheet is made, the sound crew is ready to "gather" the sounds necessary for the production.

Bells, Chimes, and Buzzers
Relatively few plays have been written that do not involve either

a telephone ring or a doorbell. Every school should have a bell board, a length of 1″ × 10″ or 12″, containing the following: a doorbell, a buzzer, a door chime, and a 6-volt transformer with a regular house plug on one side of the transformer. For each unit produced there is a separate push button with one wire to the transformer and one wire to the bell, buzzer, or chime. The bell board is carried to the place backstage from which the sound is to originate, or is kept in a central location, usually near the light-board. The board is plugged into a 110-volt outlet and, on cue, the correct button is pushed.

Sound-crew members must be able to see all of the acting area at all times because many sound cues are moves rather than oral cues. If a play lacks comic relief, just keep ringing a phone after the actor has picked up the receiver. Sound cues must be well timed. Crew members should listen to real telephones and note the length of the ring and the pause between rings. Telephone bells and doorbells can be one and the same sound, with the telephone rings shorter than the doorbell rings. Sound effects must be rehearsed for perfect timing. Just as the cast rehearses four to six weeks on lines, the sound crew should rehearse effects at least two weeks before the production. Good timing is not achieved in one or two rehearsals the week of the production.

Recordings
Today, nearly every sound that one can imagine is available on a record. Several major companies supply sound-effect records. It is best to write for a catalog rather than request a specific sound. Records usually are made with a number of sounds on one side, and a school can save money by studying the most-needed sounds on a single record. Several companies produce a "general" sound-effects record at a reasonable price.

Tapes
Sound effects also are available on tape, as well as on disc record-ings. Tapes do not scratch as do discs, and their life is considerably longer. Many publishers feature rented tapes with professional music and sound cues for certain plays.

Live Sounds
Some sound effects are best handled "live"; that is, by producing

the sound as it is needed by using the real sound rather than a recording. A gunshot happens to be one sound that is best produced live. In some states, discharging firearms of any kind, even blank guns, is forbidden by law. If a gunshot is required by the play, it is best to check with the local police department concerning these laws. The guns used in track or football work very well. Some theatrical supply houses feature inexpensive blank guns for this purpose, and it is best to buy "soft report" blanks since stages have a tendency to amplify the sound. If state law forbids the discharge of blank guns or the local community has such laws, gunshots can be produced very effectively by using a length of 1″ × 3″ (6′ or 7′ long) and placing the foot about 8″ to 10″ from its end and lifting the other end about 1½′ or 2′ off the stage floor. Keep it tight and the tension firm; then let it fly! It sounds like a shot. Door knocks, shouts, crowd noises, etc., can all be done live backstage. Be sure to rehearse them, but don't let crowd noises or shouts drown the actors' lines.

Tape Recorder and Record Player Hook-up

In Fig. 45 the method of hooking up a tape recorder and record player into the auditorium public-address system is shown. The methods offered in these illustrations are for schools *without adequate sound systems* to permit the addition of tape recorders or turntables. For schools with adequate sound systems, the methods described here are not necessary. The broken line presents an alternate method.

Here are several suggestions for using either tapes or record players:

1. Set the volume level on the public-address amplifier, not on the tape or record player. Mark the volume setting with a piece of tape.

2. Turn the P.A. volume down the instant the sound cue is finished. Don't touch it again until the next cue. The motor's running in either the tape or the record player can be picked up readily by the P.A. system. Fade the sound in at the proper moment by turning up the volume on the P.A. system. It takes practice to learn the fading in and out, but it is worth it.

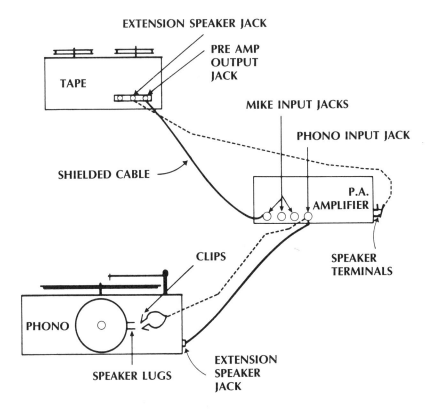

Fig. 45. Hooking up tape recorder and record player to public-address system.

3. Set the volume level on the tape recorder or record player *once* in the beginning, and don't touch it until the play is over. The tape or record player acts as a pre-amplifier for the system, and therefore the gain need not be very high.

4. Set the tone level on the P.A. and the tape or record player at about the same place. Treble rather than bass produces more accurate sound effects.

5. Practice the sounds early in rehearsals so that actors and technicians get the "feel" of sound cues. Just as the actors practice lines, the sound crew must practice sound effects.

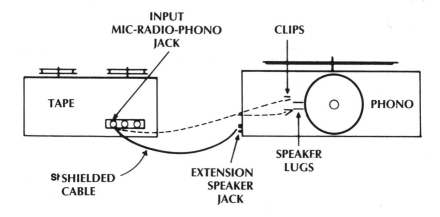

Fig. 46. Connecting a tape recorder to a record player for dubbing.

Dubbing Sounds from Record to Tape

Figure 46 illustrates two ways of connecting a tape recorder and a record player for dubbing. The broken line indicates the method to be used if the record player does not have an extension speaker jack. Sometimes it is necessary to remove several screws to gain access to the speaker lugs under the turntable. These can be replaced once the clips have been applied to the speaker lugs. The clips *must not touch each other* or the sound will be distorted with a hum.

1. Find the spot on the record where the sound effect begins, stop the record with your hand, leave the record player on so the turntable continues to spin — even though the record does not. Now *gently* turn the record back one full turn for LP records. The sound effect is now "cued." Hold the record on cue.

2. Depress the record lever on the tape recorder, and hold the tape with the pause lever or button. Volume should be set.

3. Release the pause lever and let the tape travel 6″ to 1′ at 7½ i.p.s. speed.

4. Release the cued record and record the sound effect.

5. Fade out the volume on the tape recorder when the sound effect is finished. Fade out quickly.

6. Keep the volume level on the record player low to avoid distortion.

7. Stop the tape by pulling the pause lever first; then push the stop button. Pushing the stop button first can cause a "pop" on the tape.

8. Cue the next effect. Allow about 2' of tape between the sound effects with the volume set at 0 as a leader. Some sound crews give themselves oral cues in the leader space, such as "Sound #2, Act I, car door opening." If oral cues are used, it means the sound technician will need a set of headphones to hear the cues. Still others splice in white leader tape as a means of separating sounds. It is possible to write on the white leader the data needed for the cue. If the sound crew uses the white leader with written cues, it is a good idea to keep a small flashlight or penlight handy to read the sound cues.

The development of inexpensive 8-track and cassette systems makes either or both tempting for schools to use in sound systems rather than expensive reel-to-reel tape recorders. Both the 8-track and the cassette have major disadvantages for use as sound effects recorders. First, they both travel at slow speeds as compared to reel-to-reel recorders where speed can be adjusted; second, traveling as slowly as they do, a very small space is used for the actual sound on the tape, making selections very difficult to locate and more difficult to splice. Certainly the quality of the sound is equal to that of many reel-to-reel recorders, but the disadvantages should be weighed very carefully before investing in an 8-track or cassette system. Either cassette or 8-track is fine for mood music or intermission and pre-curtain music.

Intermission and Scene Change Music

Some schools use music to cover scene changes and at intermissions to give the audience something to occupy its time.

Music can assist in creating the proper mood for a play. Further, it helps the audience relax and become more receptive to what will take place on the stage.

Pre-curtain music, played before the play starts, should be of the "mood" type, non-vocal and not the popular music of the moment. Some theatrical supply houses carry a full line of mood music for this purpose. Music should be selected that blends with the play in terms of *time* and *mood*. Many students' LP collections have music that may be suitable for pre-curtain music.

Fitting the music to the mood of the play is indeed difficult. Any director or student crew member thinking of doing this should begin the "music search" almost as soon as the play is selected for production. Many times parts of classical works serve well for climax points and provide unidentifiable themes. These blend well with many of the classic tragedies. Music used as scene change-cover also should be of the non-vocal, non-pop kind. Classics, light opera, and some of the "standards" make the best scene change-cover. Music should be dubbed at the same level as the sound effects in order to keep a constant level on the P.A. volume.

Specific Sound Effects

If a school has difficulty locating a specific sound effect, it is suggested they call on the local radio station for assistance. Most stations subscribe to a production-aids service that provides nearly every sound possible. Stations usually are willing to help school drama groups, provided they don't wait until the last minute. Be sure you provide the station with a very specific request and supply a clean tape upon which the sound effect can be recorded. Good public relations dictates that the sound technician making the request for a sound effect provide a couple of complimentary play tickets to the announcer or staff person doing the dubbing.

Finally, remember that perfection in sound effects is necessary for every production — comedy, drama, melodrama, farce, or tragedy. Practice sound effects in the early stages of production. Dub as much as possible on tape for ease of handling and reproduction. Practice timing many times on difficult cues. Be sure to keep the equipment in good operating condition and return all borrowed equipment immediately after the final performance.

ooden frame covered with muslin or canvas.

n: a drawing showing the placement of props and scenery
age.

ise into the loft, out of the audience's view.

an efficient modern spotlight, featuring a lens with con-
ircles and producing a soft-edge light.

r gels: transparent color media placed in color frame to
light color.

eries of I-beams just under the stage roof to which blocks
es are attached, through which lines (wire cable) pass to
l lower battens.

cloth: a muslin or canvas covering for the floor of the
ea, frequently painted a neutral gray or green.

row: low-profile pieces of scenery (shrubs or flowers)
hide the bottom of the sky cyc or drop.

arrow flat, usually less than 2′ wide.

e: clothesline cord used for putting flats together.

ieces of the cyc, usually 4′ to 6′ wide, hung in pairs
parallel to the act curtain, stage right and stage left, for
entrances or the backstage area from the audience's

lot: a drawing or diagram showing the placement of lighting
ents, the plugging systems, and where the light beams hit
e.

he wattage of light instruments supplied by one electrical

l platform: a folding platform 1′ to 3′ high.

an irregular shape in scenery, usually less than 6′ high,
s ground rows, building outlines, suggested walls, and
s.

nium: the "picture frame" enclosing the stage, the opening
n the stage and the audience.

to slant a setting at an angle from the audience's viewpoint.

: pieces of scenery used down right and left to mask the
age area.

ht: a lighting instrument, encased in a metal housing, that
beam of light which can be directed and adjusted toward
ge acting area.

: to take down a set or remove a prop from the stage acting

Stage and Lighting Terminolo

Act curtain: the curtain hung upsta
and closes or rises up and down at
Acting area: the portion of the stage
play.
Apron: the section of the stage betv
orchestra pit.
Asbestos: the fireproof curtain hung
closing off the stage area in case of fi
the fire-alarm system of the building. (T
use even though fireproof curtains are
material.)
Backdrop: a large piece of muslin or
the stage setting. It sometimes featur
Backing: flats or drops behind scenery
stage area.
Batten: a long piece of wood or pipe
lights are hung; also used for weightin
Border: a width of material hung across
area to hide the grid and loft from the
Border lights: rows of lamps in a long
pipes from a pipe batten above the act
Box set: a two- or three-wall setting cor
a room interior.
Brace: a jointed, adjusted, adjustable,
flats and window flats.
Cable: fourteen-two stranded wire insu
connecting lights to the switchboard.
Circuit: the complete path of electrical c
the light instrument.
Color frames: metal holders into which
and which are fitted into the front of lig
Connectors: devices for joining lighting
cables together.
Curtain line: the line on the stage floor
when it is closed.
Cyclorama or cyc: a background curtain h
of the stage.
Dimmer: an electrical instrument which
electrical current flowing to the light instr

Flat: a w
Floor pla
on the s
Fly: to i
Fresnel:
centric
Gelatin
give the
Grid: a
or shea
raise an
Ground
acting a
Ground
used to
Jog: a
Lashlin
Legs:
runnin
maskin
view.
Light
instrui
the sta
Load:
circuit
Parall
Profile
such
skylin
Prosc
betwe
Rake:
Retur
backs
Spotl
gives
the s
Strik
area.

Switchboard: the service panel that contains the switches or circuit-breakers controlling the stage lighting; sometimes contains the dimming mechanism as well.

Teaser: a short curtain hung behind the acting curtain, regulating the height of the stage opening and hiding the spotlight batten. Some stages contain three teasers. (Sometimes called *borders*; however, borders are usually fixed and do not move up and down.)

Throw: the distance from the lens of the lighting instrument to the object to be lit; most light instruments have a *limited* throw, depending upon wattage.

Wagons: platforms about 6″ high, on casters so they can be moved quietly onstage; width varies from a few feet to 10′ or 20′.

Wattage: electrical power measurement for spotlights and lamps; usually denotes capacity or rating by fire underwriters (ULA).

Suggested Activities

1. Make plans to convert a cafeteria into an arena theatre. Planning should include location of the acting area, seating plan, storage of tables and chairs, entrances and exits, make-up and costume changes, and handling the audience.

2. Plan a profile set for one of last year's plays. Draw a floor plan and a simple perspective.

3. Read the one-act dramatization of Nathaniel Hawthorne's *The Minister's Black Veil* (by Robert Brome) and plan a profile setting for it. The set should convey the period of the play.

4. Draw a floor plan for Shakespeare's *The Comedy of Errors*. Plan for scene shifts. Show on your floor plan how to accomplish these. Try color-coding the scenes.

5. Plan to add a "thrust stage" to your present stage. How can this be accomplished? Show how it can be made "portable." How can this be accomplished in an auditorium-gym combination—with basketball practice, orchestra rehearsals, etc.?

6. Make a set of model flats about 30″ or 36″ high. Construct all flats as they should be made. Paint them a neutral gray as a base coat and spatter with each color of the wheel. Plan a set using your model.

7. Make a lighting plot for Tennessee Williams' *The Glass Menagerie*. Note the special-effects lights that are required.

8. Clean and repair all lighting instruments on your stage. Check lamps in spots for "bubbles" (when the lamp is too close to the reflector the glass will mold itself to the shape of the reflector). Check all cables and connectors for loose wires and breaks. Carefully clean the lens systems with paper towels or newspaper (avoid lint left by cloth).

9. Plan a lighting demonstration for your classmates. Use the 36″ model set constructed in activity 6 to show the effects of light-color media (gels) on various set colors. Show how the light placement affects mood and meaning on the stage.

10. Work out a property list for the play *RUR* by Karel Capek. (This play can be found in a number of play collections.) Be sure to list the props by act. Make a "prop flow-chart" showing the location and placement of props on the stage. Try making up a code for props and locations.

11. Make a papier-mâché prop for Eugene lonesco's *The Bald Soprano*. Props for this play should be gaudy, surrealistic, and oversize. How else can the prop be made? With what kind of materials?

12. Plan the sound-effects cue sheet for *The Glass Menagerie*. Note the musical cues that run in and out of the entire play. Can this play be made into a dramatic non-vocal opera so that each character has a theme? Locate all suitable sound and musical effects. Make a list of the record numbers and the cut numbers on the recordings.

13. Practice dubbing sound cues with a tape recorder and record player until you can stop the instant an effect is finished.

14. Visit your local radio station to see how commercials are "cut." Ask to watch while one is being made. Check with the program director about dubbing sound effects for your play.

15. Make a model set for one of the following plays, using cardboard flats and doll furniture: *You Can't Take It with You*, *The Skin of Our Teeth*, *The Adding Machine*, *Gidget*, *Antigone*, and *Oedipus Rex*.

16. Write to several lighting companies for their catalogs. Make plans to revise your school's lighting system with one of the newer systems. Consult with your director on some of the shortcomings of the present system. Show a complete plan and cost sheet (excluding installation) for all equipment.

17. Working in pairs, measure, cut (with a handsaw), and put together a "test flat" measuring 4' × 3'. After you have made the frame, cover it with a scrap piece of muslin.

18. Collect pictures from home-furnishings magazines and show by floor plan and perspective how you could convert them into stage settings.

19. Consult a book on furniture styles from your school library or public library. Plan a demonstration on the chief characteristics of various historical periods in furniture. If your libraries do not have such a book, visit one of your town's furniture stores.

20. Make a "production work-schedule" for scenery, lighting, props, and sound effects. Show such items as when set construction begins, when painting of the set is to begin, when the lighting crew should have its plot finished, when they set lights. Get a calendar and a copy of the rehearsal schedule before you start your planning. Resolve such difficulties as rehearsals and work sessions at the same time, and other groups wanting to use the stage or the school shop. Give each crew a deadline by which work is to be completed. Plan to get large props to the school via a truck.

Bibliography

Adix, Vern. *Theatre Scenecraft.* Anchorage, Ky.: Children's Theatre Press, 1957.

Bay, Howard. *Stage Design.* New York: Drama Book Specialists, 1974.

Bellman, Williard. *Scene Design, Stage Lighting, Sound, Costume and Makeup: A Scenographic Approach.* New York: Harper & Row, 1983.

Bryson, Nicholas. *Thermoplastic Scenery for the Theatre.* New York: Drama Book Specialists, 1970.

Burris-Meyer, Harold, and Cole, Edward C. *Scenery for the Theatre*. Rev. ed. Boston: Little Brown & Co. 1975.

Burris-Meyer, Harold, et al. *Sound in the Theatre*. New York: Theatre Arts Books, 1979.

Govier, Jacquie. *Create Your Own Stage Props*. Englewood, N.J.: Prentice Hall Press, 1986.

Gruver, Bert. *The Stagemanager's Handbook*. Edited by Frank Hamilton. New York: Drama Book Specialists, 1972.

McCandless, Stanley R. *A Method of Lighting the Stage*. 4th ed. New York: Theatre Art Books, Inc., 1958.

Parker, W. Oren. *Sceno-Graphic Techniques*. 3rd ed. Carbondale, Ill.: Southern Illinois University Press, 1987.

———. *Stage Lighting Practice and Design*. New York: Holt Rinehart & Winston, 1987.

Parker, W. Oren, and Smith, Harvey K. *Scene Design and Stage Lighting*. 5th ed. New York: Holt Rinehart & Winston, 1985.

Pecktal, Lynn. *Designing and Painting for the Theatre*. New York: Holt Rinehart & Winston, 1975.

Pilbrow, Richard. *Stage Lighting*. New York: Applause Theatre Books, 1986.

Stern, Lawrence. *Stage Management: Guidebook of Practical Techniques*. 3rd ed. Boston: Allyn & Bacon, 1986.

Streader, Timothy, and Williams, John. *Create Your Own Stage Lighting*. Englewood, N.J.: Prentice Hall Press, 1986.

Thomas, Terry. *Create Your Own Stage Sets*. Englewood, N.J.: Prentice Hall Press, 1984.

Periodicals

Information about single copy and subscription rates is available from the address listed.

Theatre Crafts. Theatre Crafts, P.O. Box 630, Holmes, PA 19043–0630.

Theatre Design and Technology. U.S. Institute for Theatre Technology, 245 West 52nd Street, New York, NY 10019.

Sources of Supply

The New York Theatrical Sourcebook. Available from Broadway Press, 120 Duane Street, #407, New York, NY 10007. (This volume lists 2,500 companies who provide materials and services for the stage. It contains a listing of companies providing special effects items and machines.)

Theatre Crafts Annual Directory. Available from Theatre Crafts, P.O. Box 630, Holmes, PA 19043–0630. (Published annually, this volume contains a listing of over 1,500 products and services for the performing arts.)

NTC SPEECH AND THEATRE BOOKS

Speech Communication

THE BASICS OF SPEECH, Galvin, Cooper, & Gordon
CONTEMPORARY SPEECH, HopKins & Whitaker
CREATIVE SPEAKING, Buys et al.
CREATIVE SPEAKING SERIES
DYNAMICS OF SPEECH, Myers & Herndon
GETTING STARTED IN PUBLIC SPEAKING, Prentice & Payne
LISTENING BY DOING, Galvin
LITERATURE ALIVE! Gamble & Gamble
MEETINGS: RULES & PROCEDURES, Pohl
PERSON TO PERSON, Galvin & Book
PUBLIC SPEAKING TODAY! Prentice & Payne
SELF-AWARENESS, Ratliffe & Herman
SPEAKING BY DOING, Buys, Sill, & Beck

Theatre

ACTING AND DIRECTING, Grandstaff
THE BOOK OF CUTTINGS FOR ACTING & DIRECTING, Cassady
THE BOOK OF SCENES FOR ACTING PRACTICE, Cassady
THE DYNAMICS OF ACTING, Snyder & Drumsta
AN INTRODUCTION TO THEATRE AND DRAMA, Cassady & Cassady
PLAY PRODUCTION TODAY! Beck et al.
STAGECRAFT, Beck

 For a current catalog and information about our complete line of language arts books, write:
National Textbook Company,
a division of NTC Publishing Group
4255 West Touhy Avenue
Lincolnwood (Chicago), Illinois 60646-1975 U.S.A.

00009707